# Mark Twain

## *A Descriptive Guide to Biographical Sources*

Jason Gary Horn

The Scarecrow Press, Inc.
Lanham, Maryland, and London
1999

SCARECROW PRESS, INC.

Published in the United States of America
by Scarecrow Press, Inc.
4720 Boston Way
Lanham, Maryland 20706

4 Pleydell Gardens, Folkestone
Kent CT20 2DN, England



British Library Cataloguing in Publication Information Available

**Library of Congress Cataloging-in-Publication Data**

Horn, Jason Gary, 1951–
Mark Twain : a descriptive guide to biographical sources / Jason Gary Horn.
p. cm.
Includes bibliographical references and indexes.
ISBN 0-8108-3630-0 (alk. paper)
1. Twain, Mark, 1835–1910—Bibliography. I. Title.
Z8176.H67 1999
[PS1331] 98-54311
016.818'409—dc21 CIP

The paper used in this publication meets the minimum requirements of American National Standard for Information Sciences—Permanence of Paper for Printed Library Materials, ANSI/NISO Z39.48–1992.
Manufactured in the United States of America.

*For my wife, Sharon,*
*and my daughters, Diana and Sara*

*Photo courtesy of the*
*Mark Twain Home Foundation, Hannibal, Missouri.*

# Contents

# Preface

For many, Mark Twain himself is as much a subject for research and discussion as are his works. Students, critics, and scholars find it difficult to write about Twain's work without attending to matters of his life. Often biographers have divided Twain's life and work into periods, focusing at times on the Hannibal years, his later travels on the Western frontier, his experiences as a "respectable" novelist at Hartford, his sojourn in Europe during the 1890s, or the last decade of his life and checkered literary career. Indeed, few full-length biographies exist, and no definitive study of Twain's life has yet been written. As with other major American writers, Twain's life experiences are nearly as varied as those he created for his fictional characters. Nonetheless, taken together, the hundreds of critical and biographical studies on Twain tell his story in great detail, from many perspectives, and across numerous lines of inquiry.

The history of scholarship devoted to Twain's life and work, then, is long and rich and offers material that covers nearly every facet of the life of this popular American writer. But while much biographical matter exists, little can be found in the way of an organized guide to it. My hope is that this work will offer just that, an annotated guide to the wealth of biographical sources focusing on the life of Mark Twain. The main emphasis within each of the annotative entries is on describing the sources and not on evaluating them, unless facts are in error. Of prime concern is the scope of a particular source, its aim, and the type and extent of its documentation. Though brief, the summative entries allow those interested to approach Twain's life from varying contexts and within the limits of their own particular aims.

The scope of this guide encompasses all types of biographical material: general studies and indexes, standard and other notable biographies, autobiography, letters and journals, critical studies, and the most useful of those books and articles that significantly add to our knowledge of Mark Twain. Coverage begins with the earliest known biographical sources, including some written during the author's lifetime, and extends to the most current perceptions of Twain's life and career—a little more than a hundred years of publications about Mark Twain. Twain's reputation remains strong and new books about him surface every year. Although I have necessarily bypassed important critical works of tangential biographical importance, I have included the most recent sources that have added new and original insight into our view of Twain's life in particular. Given the confines of textual space, I have been somewhat more stingy with the choice of articles, providing a separate section for select essays that are predominantly biographical in coverage.

This book, then, is not a complete bibliographical guide; rather it is a reference work designed to aid in a particular type of study. Other notable bibliographies on Mark Twain do exist, and though none specifically targets biography or offers an annotated guide to sources relating to Twain's life and career, they fill the gaps within this work and extend the range of its findings. Thomas A. Tenney's *Mark Twain: A Reference Guide* (1977) is most important for its coverage and Tenney's astute and succinct descriptions of a vast amount of primary and secondary source material, from collections of Twain's letters, essays, and stories to a wealth of articles and books written about him. An index and chronological ordering of bibliographic entries in Tenney's work ease the researcher's task, but considerable sifting and browsing may be needed for locating specific texts. Of course, scholars have written much more about Twain since the publication of Tenney's guide in 1977; supplements to Tenney's guide can be found in *American Literary Realism* from 1977 to 1983, and to a varying degree in the *Mark Twain Circular* from 1984 to the present. The annual edition of *American Literary Scholarship* also reviews a limited number of new works published each year on Twain. Aside from these sources, selective bibliographical material can be found in Justin Kaplan's *Mark Twain, A Profile* (1967), Eugene H. Long's *The New Mark Twain Handbook* (1985), and James Wilson's *A Reader's Guide to the Short Stories of Mark Twain* (1987).

None of these sources offers a complete bibliographic survey, however, and none offers an annotated guide to the particular sources most appropriate for understanding Mark Twain's life. In the following pages, I aim to provide such a guide, a reference map to the large number of primary and secondary sources that contain the story of the man we know as Mark Twain.

# Acknowledgments

Let me thank Frank Roberts, first of all, who acted as a sounding board for my early ideas for this book. His knowledge as a reference librarian and writer helped shape this book in its proposal stages, and his bibliographical work on James Michener sparked my initial interest in doing a similar project. Likewise, I was inspired by the work of Robert B. Harmon, whose reference book on John Steinbeck provided me with a model of scholarship.

I was fortunate enough to receive valuable editorial help in the course of compiling this book. Without Julie Schroeder and Susan Ferber, this book would still be in process and in unpolished form. My appreciation goes out to both women, whose sense of language and provocative editorial suggestions, along with a talent for effective designing, carried this book to completion in a timely manner.

Time matters whenever a book is in progress, and without the help of some dedicated librarians I would not have met my necessary deadlines. At Gordon College, the staff members at Hightower Library eased my scholarly work by directing me toward the most useful sources and through the intricacies of on-line computer searches. Beverly Eskridge, Rebecca Hamilton, Linda Appleby, and Diane Hollingsworth were especially generous with their time and patience. Many of the sources I examined were difficult to find, some were in special or restricted holdings, and some were out of print, but Beth Pye kept the interlibrary loan process moving smoothly and was able to track down even the oldest and dustiest of books. Nancy Anderson kept (and keeps) the library filled with the newest of books, which enabled me to stay as current as possible. I am indebted as well to library staff members at Mercer University, Auburn University, Georgia State University, and the University of Georgia, who all helped along the way.

The staff, faculty, and administration at Gordon College were equally supportive. William Thurman offered his early support and helped provide the time necessary for research. F. Brett Cox was kind enough to lend me some rare books that included little-known recollections of Twain. His discussions about Twain and American literature in general, along with the conversations I enjoyed with Susan Hendricks, Anna Dunlap Higgins, and Mary Alice Money, kept my spirits high and enthusiasm centered on the project at hand. Bill Day and Gloria Henderson patiently listened to my publication concerns, while Rhonda Wilcox and Edward Whitelock were always on hand with their knowledge of editing and effective presentation. And without the coordinating efforts of Betty Niblett, our division staff assistant, we of the faculty may have found little time to discuss much at all.

Dr. Jerry Williamson, president of Gordon College, warmly supported my research and enabled and encouraged me to pursue my study within the framework of my teaching duties. The many conversations we shared about the lives of American authors, and Twain in particular, enabled me to refine my notions of biography and my sense of any one writer's significance. His support, as with that of Dr. Andrea Hardin, kept my spirits high.

I cannot forget to mention my two daughters, Diana and Sara, and their patience with a father who spends an inordinate amount of time thinking and writing about Mark Twain. My wife, Sharon, has also gracefully endured my affair with this book and the hours it has demanded. My hope is that its readers find the time to have been well spent.

1

# Dictionaries and Encyclopedias

*While not always providing in-depth knowledge, certain reference works remain valuable tools for a general introduction to an author. To a greater or lesser degree, these reference sources provide useful dates, facts, and interpretations and establish an author's significance in history and literature. The following entries refer to the dictionaries and encyclopedias that offer just such a range of coverage.*

## GENERAL DICTIONARIES AND ENCYCLOPEDIAS

Since these more general works provide basic biographical facts in short entry form and are often the product of editorial collaboration, entries in this chapter are arranged alphabetically by title.

1. *Academic American Encyclopedia.* Danbury, Conn.: Grolier, 1992.

   Twain's entry appears on page 357 of volume 19 of this set. H. G. Baetzhold, a notable Twain scholar, writes a straightforward account of Twain's life, supplying the reader with a substantial set of facts and dates. Baetzhold offers little in the way of interpretation but does suggest that recent facts about Twain's later years challenge assumptions about the author's failing artistic powers. As Baetzhold puts it, the later period "was not the wasteland described by some critics."

2. *American Authors and Books, 1640 to the Present Day.* Edited and compiled by William J. Burke and Will D. Howe. 3d edition revised by Irving Weiss and Anne Weiss. New York: Crown Publishers, 1972.

   The editors call this text an "encyclopedic distillation of the national culture" for "occasional or curious readers" and researchers. The *Clemens* entry appears on page 123, with birth and death and book publication dates, along with a list of major critical and biographical studies; the *Twain* entry, on page 625, is mostly a note on his use of a pen name.

3. *The American Heritage College Dictionary.* 3d edition. Boston: Houghton Mifflin Company, 1993.

   This general dictionary prides itself on its clear and readable presentation. The entry for Mark Twain is found under *Clemens* on page 261 and indicates his birth and death dates and his best-known work.

4. *Cambridge Biographical Dictionary.* Edited and compiled by Magnus Magnussen. Cambridge: Cambridge University Press, 1990.

   The first edition of this reference book was published in 1897, and the editors of this edition, like those of the first, aim to recognize the "little somebodies" as well as the "great nobodies." Given its broad scope, this volume offers only short entries, yet provides the "essential outline" of each subject's life and achievement. With Twain, however, the volume offers little in the way of specific information beyond the year 1889 and the publication of *A Connecticut Yankee in King Arthur's Court.* Twain's entry is found on pages 1482–83.

5. *The Cambridge Dictionary of American Biography.* Edited and compiled by John S. Bowman. New York: Cambridge University Press, 1995.

   A highly readable sourcebook that covers the major occupations, professions, and activities of important Americans. It offers over nine thousand entries, and there are two indexes for finding particular subjects, one listing entries by occupation and the other by name. The entry for *Clemens, Samuel Langhorne,* is on page 138 and offers mostly a list of key facts and noteworthy events, all of which lead eventually to the conclusion that Twain ended his life and career as a dark and brooding man.

6. *Cassell's Encyclopedia of World Literature.* Edited and compiled by S. H. Steinberg. 3 vols. New York: William Morrow and Company, 1973.

   Intended as a quick reference source, this compilation provides an overview of Twain's life and career on page 125. Although few dates are given along the way, the entry does include some assessment of Twain scholarship through the date of the volume's publication and a bibliography of the author's major books.

7. *Collier's Encyclopedia* with Bibliography and Index. 24 vols. New York: Macmillan Educational Company, 1997.

These volumes are aimed at scholars, serious students, and adults who need a brief but substantial source of information about a topic of interest. The articles are generally written by authorities and offer a wide range of coverage of individual topics. A bibliography for the encyclopedia as a whole is located in a separate volume. DeLancey Ferguson, author of *Mark Twain: Man and Legend,* provides Twain's article on pages 558–60 in volume 22. After citing important dates in Twain's life (those for his birth, death, occupations, and publications), Ferguson divides the information into four sections: a general biography, then a discussion of major works, followed by an analysis of major achievements, and finally a note on major biographical and critical scholarship. A photograph accompanies the entry.

8. *The Encyclopedia Americana: International Edition.* 30 vols. Danbury, Conn.: Grolier, 1997.

This encyclopedia attempts to bridge the gap between the scholar and the general reader by providing more than fifty thousand entries, all of which are accurate and clearly written to satisfy a wide-ranging audience. This is the first major encyclopedia to be published in the United States, and its extensive reach and authoritative collection of contributors confirms its continuing competency and popularity. James M. Cox, one of the more notable Twain scholars, supplies the information on Twain on pages 291a–291d. Cox covers Twain's life in general in the first section, his major achievements in the second section, then devotes the last section to a discussion of Twain's art. He includes a photograph of an older Twain and a short but useful bibliography.

9. *Merriam-Webster's Encyclopedia of Literature.* Edited and compiled by Kathleen Kuiper. Springfield, Mass.: Merriam-Webster, 1995.

This volume is densely packed with facts, and Twain's entry, found on page 1140, offers a quick reference to a wealth of information relating to his life and career. It includes cross-references that key facts and events to specific works.

10. *The New Encyclopaedia Britannica.* 15th ed. 32 vols. Chicago: Encyclopaedia Britannica, 1992.

    This is one of the oldest and most reputable general encyclopedias in the English language. Its first set of volumes, the micropaedia, provides standard information on its topics; the second set of volumes, the macropaedia, provides more in-depth consideration of select subjects. The entry on Twain on pages 75–77 of the micropaedia, though short, reviews the major events in his life, beginning with a section on his Hannibal, Missouri, youth and early travels. The unsigned article continues with its coverage of Twain's travels and mature writings and concludes with a consideration of the author's financial difficulties and last years. A two-volume index points to other entries that note Twain's places of residence and personal relationships. The main entry includes a photograph of an older Twain.

11. *Webster's New Biographical Dictionary.* Springfield, Mass.: Merriam-Webster, 1988.

    The entry for Twain appears on page 216 and provides a succinct review of significant dates in Twain's life and career. The entry includes the publication dates of Twain's major titles.

12. *The World Book Encyclopedia.* 22 vols. Chicago: World Book, 1997.

    Designed primarily for elementary, junior high, and high school students, this general encyclopedia presents its material in both an entertaining and informative format. Entries are factual and accurate but not overly burdened with dates. Illustrations abound. The entry on Twain, on pages 528–30, begins with a section on the author's early life and journalistic years, through 1866; next comes a section on Twain's most successful years, through 1889 and the publication of *A Connecticut Yankee in King Arthur's Court;* and the final section covers his later years and death. The entry includes several photographs. A separate volume provides an index and research guide.

# BIOGRAPHICAL DICTIONARIES AND ENCYCLOPEDIAS

The following dictionaries and encyclopedias focus on particular authors and subjects and are generally products of only one or two writers or compilers. The entries in this section are arranged alphabetically by last names.

13. Adams, Oscar Fay. *A Dictionary of American Authors.* 4th ed. Boston: Houghton, Mifflin and Company, 1901.

    Those interested in the life of Mark Twain may find this book more curious than useful. It provides no dates for the publication of Twain's works or for the events of his life, though the volume mentions a few of the books and events for which he is now known. Adams praises Twain as a "celebrated humorist," recognizes his success and popularity, but notes that "only a very small portion of his writing has any place in literature."

14. Bain, Robert, Joseph M. Flora, and Louis D. Rubin Jr., editors. *Southern Writers: A Biographical Dictionary.* Baton Rouge: Louisiana State University Press, 1979.

    Designed to give "brief and informative sketches of lives of authors associated with the American South," this single volume contains entries on 379 such writers. Claiming Twain as one of them, Arlin Turner delivers his sketch of the author on pages 85–89. Turner emphasizes Twain's love/hate relationship with the South as he links biographical facts to the author's early work, in particular. Turner includes a thorough bibliography of Twain's published books.

15. Gale, Robert L. *The Gay Nineties in America: A Cultural Dictionary of the 1890s.* Westport, Conn.: Greenwood Press, 1992.

    The brief entry for Twain on pages 369–70 reviews important facts and figures in the author's life, with an emphasis on his activities during the last decade of the nineteenth century. Offered are exact dates for Twain's many occupations and places of residence, his lecture tours, travels, and the publication of his major works. The point is to reveal Twain as "obviously very unsettled." The entry also provides a list of Twain's friends and literary acquaintances as it locates him within an unusually turbulent decade of American history.

16. Johnson, Allen, and Dumas Malone. *Dictionary of American Biography: Authors Edition.* Vol. 4. New York: Charles Scribner's Sons, 1930.

Since its earliest days of publication in 1928, the *Dictionary of American Biography* has continued to be what its editors claim: a "preeminent retrospective reference work." Supplements continue to expand upon the original series of twenty books as they maintain the original focus on extraordinary individuals who have made a lasting mark on life in North America. Each entry provides basic biographical matter on the birth and death dates of its target individual as well as names of the individual's closest relatives and friends, places of residence, and dates for major events in the subject's life. The contributors for each entry also discuss the "circumstances and influences that shaped the careers of the biographees." The entry on Twain is on pages 192–98; it mainly emphasizes the life experiences that were crucial to the development of Twain's style.

17. Pizer, Donald, and Earl N. Harbett, editors. *American Realists and Naturalists.* Vol. 12 of *Dictionary of Literary Biography.* Detroit: Gale Research Company, 1982.

In general, this volume concentrates on a loosely allied group of writers who find a common bond in their attempt to disclose the unvarnished truth. Few writers can be that easily pegged, of course, and Twain's name appears under different classifications in other volumes of the *DLB.* Hamlin Hill provides the essay for this volume on pages 71–94, significantly under *Clemens, S. L.,* rather than under *Twain,* the name Pascal Covici uses in his *DLB* entry for American humorists. Hill's is a sober account, in which Twain emerges a "realist in his language and a naturalist in his final philosophy," but by temperament an "arch romantic." Hill's and Covici's essays work as companion pieces supplying a substantial amount of biographical detail and filling in gaps left by each scholar.

18. Richards, Robert Fulton, editor. *Concise Dictionary of American Authors.* New York: Philosophical Library, 1955.

The entries in this volume are designed more for students and general readers than for scholars. Each constructs a somewhat seamless narrative for the subject at hand. Twain's article, on pages 228–31, reviews facts about the author's family and early years that have been questioned, though not entirely refuted, since the publication of this volume. Richards's intention is to provide more than just facts about his subjects; in Twain's entry, he offers an analysis of Twain's writing style and content.

19. Trachtenberg, Stanley, editor. *American Humorists, 1800–1950.* Vol. 11 of *Dictionary of Literary Biography.* Detroit: Gale Research Company, 1982.

Most of the essays in this two-book volume are of substantial length, and Twain's is no exception. Written by Pascal Covici Jr., Twain's essay is in book 2, on pages 526–55. Covici first provides facts and information about Twain's life—for example, dates for birth and death, marriage, special awards, book publications—then carefully discusses his major works and significant literary acquaintances. Throughout the essay, Covici makes a concerted effort to clarify some of the most confusing periods of Twain's life. Covici includes illustrations and a select bibliography of criticism.

## AUTHOR AND SUBJECT ENCYCLOPEDIAS

20. Gale, Steven H., editor. *Encyclopedia of American Humorists.* New York: Garland Publishing, 1988.

Each entry in this "comprehensive and up-to-date reference text" is highly detailed and meticulously constructed. As a whole, the encyclopedia covers 135 authors from the colonial period to the date of its publication. Each author's entry supplies necessary biographical data for its subject and a scholarly analysis of his or her place in the tradition of American literature, particularly as a humorist. David E. E. Sloane, author of *Mark Twain as Literary Comedian* (1979), supplies the evaluative essay for Twain on pages 83–91. As a reference source, this book provides information often left out of similar texts. For example, Twain's entry includes details about his correspondence with publishers and his involvement with the establishment of copyright laws.

21. Garraty, John A., editor. *Encyclopedia of American Biography.* New York: Harper and Row, Publishers, 1974.

This encyclopedia aims to describe and evaluate the lives and contributions of noteworthy Americans. Offering more than just facts and figures, it provides "informed opinion" about the reasons behind events and actions. Each entry is divided into two sections, with the first providing a factual summary of the life and career of its subject and the second an evaluation and interpretation of his or her importance. James M. Cox, a respected Twain scholar, supplies Twain's entry on pages 200–202 (listed under *Clemens*). Echoing some of his subject's own humor, Cox clearly connects the major events in Twain's life to a career that may owe its beginnings to the author's criminal background, his desertion from the Confederate army, escape to Nevada, and eventual adoption of a pen name.

22. Herzberg, Max J. *The Reader's Encyclopedia of American Literature.* New York: Thomas Y. Crowell Company, 1962.

One of the most comprehensive reference sources for its time, this encyclopedia provides a two-part entry for each subject. Twain's entry, found on pages 1159–62, begins with a section that covers important facts about his life and career and his different types of writings. The next section includes a selection of critical comments about Twain's life and works. Renowned Twain scholars write both sections of the entry. Twain's later years and writings are generally ignored, however. Includes a cross-reference that locates Twain's major works within the context of events that shaped his life.

23. Magill, Frank N., editor. *Cyclopedia of World Authors.* 5 vols. Pasadena, Calif.: Salem Press, 1989.

In her entry for Mark Twain, Janet Lorenz outlines the major events in Twain's life, beginning with birth and death dates, and lists his principal works by genre. She offers some critical discussion of key works, providing a paragraph each for *The Adventures of Tom Sawyer* and *Adventures of Huckleberry Finn,* and singles out significant secondary studies. The entry is found in volume 5, pages 2042–43. Lorenz includes a select bibliography of critical studies and Twain biographies.

24. Murphy, Bruce, editor. *Benét's Reader's Encyclopedia.* 4th ed. New York: HarperCollins, 1996.

This book has been a standard reference work since its first publication in 1948. It contains thousands of entries covering biographies of authors, summaries of literary works, descriptions of characters, explications of literary terms, and much more. With this new edition of William Benét's comprehensive work, Murphy incorporates the latest scholarship and interpretations. The short entry for Twain is brief, factual, and accurate. It appears on pages 1052–53 and accounts for Twain's various occupations and travels as well as the central events of his life.

25. Perkins, George, Barbara Perkins, and Philip Leininger, editors. *Benét's Reader's Encyclopedia of American Literature.* New York: HarperCollins, 1991.

This may indeed be the "most comprehensive one-volume reference book in its field," as its editors claim. Its range extends beyond just the United States to embrace the literature of Canada and Latin America. Each entry integrates details on individual authors with relevant historical background, weaving the life and work of writers into the social, religious, political, and philosophical events of their time. Twain's entry appears on pages 1068–72 and is particularly valuable for understanding Twain as a part of his age.

26. Snodgrass, Mary Ellen. *Encyclopedia of Frontier Literature.* Santa Barbara, Calif.: ABC–CLIO, 1997.

This is a specialized encyclopedia that aims to define and exemplify the enormous amount of literature that centers on "the exploration and settlement of North America" by presenting that literature's history, major titles, themes, genres, and characters. Each article includes cross-references that make connections within this study of a complex network of literatures. A brief survey of Twain's life and career, which focuses on his frontier writings, appears on pages 361–66. *Roughing It* is singled out for its own entry and discussion on page 326. Particularly useful for an initial foray into Twain's frontier experience, this source includes study aids in an appendix that also provides a chronology of frontier literature from 1532 forward and a list of major frontier works and authors.

2

# Guides, Companions, and Related Reference Books

*The following reference books offer information on selected authors and subjects, and often locate them in a historical or thematic context. The depth and breadth of coverage varies with each source, but taken together these books develop a wide range of perspectives on Mark Twain's life and career.*

27. Bain, Robert, and Joseph M. Flora. *Fifty Southern Writers before 1900: A Bio-Bibliographical Sourcebook.* New York: Greenwood Press, 1987.

    This book serves as a companion volume to *Fifty Southern Writers after 1900.* Its range extends from 1607 to approximately 1900, and the entries cover those authors, from Captain John Smith to Charles W. Chesnutt, who address southern issues. Each essay on an individual author contains five parts: biographical sketch, discussion of major themes, assessment of scholarship, chronological list of works, and bibliography of selected criticism. The well-known Twain scholar Everett Emerson treats Twain in an extensive essay on pages 144–64.

28. Beacham, Walton. *Research Guide to Biography and Criticism.* 2 vols. Washington, D.C.: Research Publishing, 1985.

    This is a guide for students who are just beginning to explore research topics and for the librarians who may be helping them. It provides a quick access to those authors most likely to be assigned as research subjects. Twain's entry appears on pages 1202–6 and includes a chronological listing of the major events in his life and publication dates for his principal works. Henry J. Linburg, the entry's writer, briefly evaluates a few of Twain's most significant biographies and available autobiographical material. Aimed at improving the research range of all students, this text focuses on the most generally available information.

29. Boris, Ford. *American Literature.* Vol. 9 of *The New Pelican Guide to English Literature.* New York: Penguin Books, 1991.

The Pelican paperback series provides a convenient guide to literature in English, with volumes on the literature of Scotland, Ireland, and Wales as well as that of America, Australia, and Africa. Not necessarily aimed at scholars and critics but rather at the general reader who simply enjoys reading, this guide provides a general historical discussion of English literature as well as relevant surveys of social and cultural contexts, themes, and characteristics. Its appendix provides essential facts, a bibliography, and a list of other books that expand upon the exploration of English literature. Eric Mottram writes the entry for Mark Twain, which appears on pages 166–83; Mottram skips back and forth across the author's career, providing bits of information rather than an organized overview of Twain's life. He reviews the major critical assessments of Twain's life and work, and he provides some rare anecdotes about the author.

30. Drabble, Margaret, editor. *The Oxford Companion to English Literature.* 5th ed. New York: Oxford University Press, 1985.

This is one of the more accurate and up-to-date reference sources. It relies on the latest scholarship for the dates surrounding events in each author's life. Twain's life is factually accounted for in a few brief pages, 1018–19, from information gleaned from critical studies aimed at understanding that life and the literary works that were so much a part of it. The entry for Twain notes the editorial mishandling of the *Mysterious Stranger* manuscripts, for instance, which more substantial entries in larger reference works overlook. A brief but highly reliable source, it includes a concluding chronology that situates authors and their works in the context of world events.

31. Ehrlich, Eugene, and Gorton Carruth. *The Oxford Illustrated Literary Guide to the United States.* New York: Oxford University Press, 1982.

This text offers a wealth of biographical detail in bits and pieces, and it is organized to "help travelers find places associated with the lives and works of writers." The editors give special mention to Twain in the preface, noting that he is a particularly apt example of the restlessness of American writers. Tracing Twain's footsteps was a "staggering task," as the editors note, but his name emerges frequently within dozens of discussions. Details vary in substance, but more often than not the information is exact, as with the facts surrounding Twain's work as a printer at 167 Walnut Street in Cincinnati, Ohio, while boarding just a few blocks away at 76 Walnut Street. When possible, the editors supply current information about notable locations.

32. Fox, Richard Wightman, and James T. Kloppenberg. *A Companion to American Thought.* Cambridge, Mass.: Blackwell Publishers, 1995.

    The brief portrait found on pages 692–94 of this text presents Twain as representative of many Americans at the end of the nineteenth century. For Wightman and Kloppenberg, this means examining the details of Twain's life that point to "unresolved contradictions" about money, race, morality, and bourgeois society in general. Their account leaves Twain unable to resolve his "complex and contradictory feelings."

33. Hart, James D, editor. *The Oxford Companion to American Literature.* 6th ed. New York: Oxford University Press, 1995.

    Hart offers a straightforward factual outline of Twain's literary career and the major events in his life. Twain's entry, on page 414, also offers a brief discussion on the history of the author's pseudonym.

34. Kamm, Antony. *Biographical Companion to Literature in English.* Lanham, Md.: Scarecrow Press, 1997.

    This text is a revised and updated version of *Collins' Biographical Dictionary of English Literature.* Making connections between an author's life and work, it offers a short outline that includes major achievements in each. Although the entries are necessarily brief—1,544 authors are covered—all important dates and events are noted with cross-references and bibliographical sources that further delineate the contours of an author's career. The entry on Twain, found on pages 556–57, is surprisingly specific, to the point of listing such facts as the author's royalty payments and the total debt before his bankruptcy.

35. Kamp, Jim. *Reference Guide to American Literature.* 3d ed. Detroit: St. James Press, 1994.

More inclusive than previous volumes, this edition contains entries on 555 authors as it attempts to seamlessly integrate information about the lesser-known authors with the most famous ones. Each entry provides a brief set of facts about a writer, a complete list of the writer's published books, a select list of relevant bibliographies and critical studies, and a signed critical essay by a recognized authority on the subject at hand. John C. Gerber supplies the essay for Mark Twain. A concluding chronology for all the entries places the writers and their works within a social, cultural, and historical context.

36. Kunitz, Stanley J., and Howard Haycraft. *American Authors, 1600–1900.* New York: H. W. Wilson Company, 1938.

Contains thirteen hundred biographical entries and four hundred portraits of three centuries of American authors. Although this text is outdated, it is still useful as a starting point for biographical study and, as its editors note, "serves as a 'handy' sourcebook for both major and minor American authors." While entries are understandably brief, given the coverage, they nonetheless work to integrate critical responses into career summaries. Mark Twain is covered on pages 159–61, in an entry that draws heavily upon critical portraits of Twain as a split personality and mass of contradictions.

37. McCarthy, Joseph F. X., editor. *Record of America: A Reference History of the United States.* Vol. 2. New York: Charles Scribner's Sons, 1974.

This book is part of a ten-volume series that provides a "ready reference work" to all periods of American history and is aimed primarily at high school students and freshman and sophomore college students. The series as a whole provides an extensive reference source for an initial investigation into the life and history of the United States. Ample documentation and cross-references extend and link the information found in entries. The brief sketch on Twain, found on pages 41–42, provides the basic facts of his life and sets him in the context of other writers. The entry's contributor ranks Twain with Melville, Thoreau, and Whitman as one of America's finest writers.

38. Pollard, Arthur, editor. *Webster's New World Companion to English and American Literature.* New York: World Publishing, 1973.

This reference book briefly relates significant events in Twain's life and offers short summaries of his major works. Particularly useful is the way this volume locates Twain's career within the context of the careers of other literary talents of his time, suggesting ways in which Twain was and was not a part of literary groups or movements. The article on Twain is found on pages 686–90.

39. Rood, Karen L. *American Literature Almanac: From 1608 to the Present: An Original Compendium of Facts and Anecdotes about Literary Life in the United States of America.* New York: Bruccoli Clark Layman, 1988.

This volume provides quick access to the facts and figures surrounding the lives of American authors. In the spirit of earlier almanacs, such as Ben Franklin's, this almanac provides "interesting reading matter as well as useful facts." This means that the facts concerning any one author are scattered throughout the volume; for Twain, this is certainly the case. While Rood devotes some of the front matter to an overview of American literature, discussing certain recurring topics and prevailing subject matter, she devotes most of the text to individual authors, believing that "literary history is literary biography." Twain's main entry, with the basic facts and dates, appears on page 138. More information, however, appears in different sections of the book: in "Finales," which provides burial sites, epitaphs, last words, and deathbed works of authors, and in "Eccentric Writers," which accounts for Twain's actions as a trickster and practical joker.

40. Salzman, Jack, editor. *The Cambridge Handbook of American Literature.* New York: Cambridge University Press, 1986.

This compact handbook offers a concise review of American authors and their works. It is factual and informative rather than critical and discursive. Twain's entry, on pages 47–48, briefly surveys the author's major works in relation to significant incidents in his life. The handbook emphasizes biographical and bibliographical information.

41. Stapleton, Michael. *The Cambridge Guide to English Literature.* New York: Cambridge University Press, 1983.

This guide covers more than a thousand years of English literature, from its beginnings through the third quarter of the twentieth century. Thus, each entry in this guide offers only a brief review of facts and important dates for its subject, including the dates of honors, occupations, events, and book publications. Twain's entry, on pages 900–901, singles him out as one of America's greatest writers, in addition to providing notes on his occupations and the important facts of his life. The entry also includes an evaluation of Twain's contribution to English literature as a whole.

42. Unger, Leonard, editor in chief. *American Writers: A Collection of Literary Biographies.* Vol. 4. New York: Charles Scribner's Sons, 1974.

Published previously in the *University of Minnesota Pamphlets on American Writers* series, this essay collection is aimed at a wide audience, including high school and college students, scholars, and general readers. All ninety-seven essays provide an overview of an author's life with critical commentary on career achievements. On pages 190–213, Lewis Leary's essay on Twain focuses on integrating the author's best-known works into the major events that helped to shape them. Leary includes a select but wide-ranging bibliography.

43. Vinson, James, editor. *Novelists and Prose Writers.* New York: St. Martin's Press, 1979.

Part of the *Great Writers of the English Language* series, this book supplies authoritative essays on hundreds of major writers. John C. Gerber, a respected Twain scholar, writes the entry for Mark Twain. His evaluation of Twain's work and life is preceded by a biography section, a complete list of Twain's published books, and a select list of bibliographies and critical studies.

## 3

# Biographies

*Though no definitive story of Mark Twain's life exists, some biographies have become standard sources of information; others offer remarkable insight by providing biographical pieces that work to complete the often puzzling life and literary career of Mark Twain. Whether attempting a comprehensive sweep of Twain's life, or narrating that life in relation to particular people and places or to literary and intellectual pursuits, the Twain biographies recall why the author's life was and still is so open to interpretation. Mark Twain's life was full, rich, and often complex and contradictory. His biographies can be the same, though some are broader, some more complicated, and some more complete than others. The following entries represent sources that vary in the amount of information they offer but, taken together, represent substantial starting points from which one can begin to understand Mark Twain.*

44. Allen, Jerry. *The Adventures of Mark Twain.* Boston: Little, Brown and Company, 1954.

    This book concentrates on Twain's early and middle years, giving only scattered details on the last two decades of the author's life. Mixing facts with narrative techniques, Allen vividly weaves select documents—Twain's notebooks, autobiography, and love letters, in particular—into a fabric of events to tell a highly readable story. Allen includes a detailed index but supplies only a few general notes for his sources and no substantial documentation for his facts.

45. Baldanza, Frank. *Mark Twain: An Introduction and Interpretation.* New York: Barnes and Noble, 1961.

    This is an introductory text for students and general readers. It provides a succinct and complete survey of Twain's life that takes into account the biographical research that had been done on the author since Albert Bigelow Paine's Twain biography. To correlate Twain's works with major events in his life, Baldanza arranges the book around two key opening chapters, "The Man" and "The

Writer," then follows with chapters that link particular types of writing—travel, historical, and polemical, for instance—to Twain's career.

46. Bellamy, Gladys. *Mark Twain as a Literary Artist.* Norman: University of Oklahoma Press, 1950.

As a literary biography, this book explores Twain's creative life and the personality that surfaces through his work. Bellamy presents relevant contextual matter for understanding the development of Twain's creative efforts as she unearths the humorist and pessimist, moralist and thinker, romantic, dreamer, and genius. She wishes to avoid entering the controversy over Twain's artistic success and aims rather to examine the type of personality that nurtures conflicting interpretations. Bellamy's wide-ranging work sets the standard for studies that would continue to address the distinctive elements of Twain's personality.

47. Brashear, Minnie M. *Mark Twain: Son of Missouri.* Chapel Hill: University of North Carolina Press, 1934.

This is one of the first biographies that presents Twain as a product of his time and place and as positively influenced by his midwestern background. It details life in Hannibal, Missouri, during Twain's childhood years and provides insight into his relationship with family members. Brashear recounts the first twenty-six years of Twain's life, from 1835 to 1861, and provides a clear introduction to the Hannibal years and Twain's careers as printer and editor. Brashear includes a chapter on Twain's reading and a select but wide-ranging bibliography.

48. Brooks, Van Wyck. *The Ordeal of Mark Twain.* New York: E. P. Dutton and Company, 1920.

Although Brooks's book is not a biography proper, it serves as a provocative psychological portrait. Within his Freudian framework, Brooks constructs an artistically incomplete Twain, a man and mind suffering from a lack of intellectual nurturing and the moral strictures of a genteel culture. This portrait of a frustrated and fragmented personality sets a point of departure for numerous accounts of Twain's life.

49. Budd, Louis J. *Our Mark Twain.* Philadelphia: University of Pennsylvania Press, 1983.

    This book serves as a biography of Twain's public self. Budd gives an account of Twain's life as he shaped it for public consumption and as reporters and interviewers continued to reshape it. Budd provides a wealth of journalistic items about Twain, both factual and fanciful, and numerous photographs and illustrations of the author as he posed for magazines and newspapers.

50. Clemens, Clara. *My Father, Mark Twain. Illustrated from Family Photographs with Hitherto Unpublished Letters of Mark Twain.* New York: Harper and Brothers, 1931.

    Clemens develops her biography largely around a selection of her father's letters, those mostly to her mother and herself, dating from 1868 to 1909. Highly devotional and peppered with loving descriptions of Twain as father and husband, this work offers genuine insight into Twain's private life; at the same time, it offers an intimate portrait of the Clemens family at home in Hartford, Connecticut; New York City; and abroad in such places as Australia, India, England, France, Austria, Italy, and South Africa. Not indexed.

51. Clemens, Cyril. *My Cousin Mark Twain.* Emmaus, Pa.: Rodale Press, 1939.

    In this account of Twain's life, Clemens relies heavily upon anecdotes to tell the story of his third cousin twice removed. The rapid pace and loosely chronological structure of the book makes for entertaining reading but a patchwork biography. Some of the chapters are more detailed than others; the most biographically useful are "Some Friends of Mark Twain" and "With Mark Twain in Europe." The book is only partially documented, though Clemens provides a short index to relevant names and places.

52. Clemens, Will M. *Mark Twain: His Life and Work, A Biographical Sketch.* San Francisco: Clemens Publishing Company, 1892.

    This is the first biographical book published on Mark Twain. A mixture of fact and fiction, it selectively records events that recall and partially create Twain as a representative American success figure. It differs at points with Albert Bigelow Paine's later official biography of Mark Twain.

53. Cox, Clinton. *Mark Twain: America's Humorist, Dreamer, Prophet.* New York: Scholastic, 1995.

This straightforward account of Twain's entire life is directed toward a young audience, and it moves chronologically through the facts with little attempt at interpretation or commentary. Cox provides an ample supply of photographs of Twain and his family and friends, as well as prints and illustrations of historical scenes and events surrounding the author's travels and various occupations. There are no source citations, but the bibliography is concise and the index thorough.

54. Daugherty, Charles Michael. *Samuel Clemens.* Illustrated by Kurt Werth. New York: Thomas Y. Crowell Company, 1970.

This book serves as a Mark Twain primer for children. It presents a surprising amount of facts over its short length as it traces the formative years of Sam Clemens. The book concludes with young Clemens's debut as Mark Twain, the writer.

55. De Voto, Bernard. *Mark Twain's America.* Boston: Little, Brown and Company, 1932.

Although this work could be classified as a biography, De Voto labels it as a corrective portrait. It is an account of Twain's life aimed at countering *The Ordeal of Mark Twain,* Van Wyck Brooks's earlier and influential account of the author as a literary underachiever and a victim of inhibiting circumstances. Clinging tenaciously to the facts about Twain's frontier experience, De Voto presents Twain as essentially connected to his early environment. This work provides valuable details on Twain's growth as a frontier humorist and folk artist. It concludes with what might be considered Twain's initiation into Eastern gentility, the ill-received Whittier birthday speech.

56. De Voto, Bernard. *Mark Twain at Work.* Cambridge: Harvard University Press, 1942.

De Voto approaches Twain from two directions in this book of three essays. In the first two essays, he turns to Twain's talents as a writer for a discussion of his working habits. In the final essay, "The Symbols of Despair," De Voto brings to light new information on Twain's final years and digs deeper into the psychology that orchestrated the author's life and working habits. De Voto makes it a point to disassociate himself from Van Wyck Brooks and his followers, however, referring to his analysis of the "unconscious portions" of Twain's mind as a "report only"—not as a Freudian evaluation of some debilitating mental condition but as a description of Twain's mind at work.

57. Eaton, Jeanette. *America's Own Mark Twain.* New York: William Morrow and Company, 1958.

A useful biography for young readers, this book accounts for some of the major events in Mark Twain's life and reviews some of his major works.

58. Emerson, Everett. *The Authentic Mark Twain: A Literary Biography of Samuel L. Clemens.* Philadelphia: University of Pennsylvania Press, 1984.

Emerson draws an image- and career-conscious Twain capable of being, in response to a particular moment or audience, either authentic or highly pretentious. Focusing on Twain's involvement with his writing, this biography evenly treats the entire range of Twain's work. Emerson unearths Twain the artist and businessman, bringing to light his artistic concerns with style, dreams, and inspiration within the framework of his pragmatic working habits and enterprising literary maneuvers. This book draws upon some previously unpublished material, mostly letters, and concludes with an extensive bibliography of published and unpublished material.

59. Ferguson, DeLancey. *Mark Twain, Man and Legend.* Indianapolis: The Bobbs-Merrill Company, 1943.

Written for the scholar and general reader, this full-length biographical study focuses primarily on Twain as a "literary person." While unraveling Twain's literary life, Ferguson attends closely to the evolving complications the author experienced as a writer, from his early tales to his late attempts at creative autobiography. Working from all available sources, Ferguson presents facts that reflect his own careful study of a wide and substantial range of scholarship.

60. Geismar, Maxwell. *Mark Twain: An American Prophet.* Boston: Houghton Mifflin Company, 1970.

This book challenges earlier critical claims about Twain's split personality and its detrimental effect upon his literary career by closely examining available autobiographical material. Leaning occasionally on Freud but more often on the psychological theories of Otto Rank, Geismar depicts Twain as an artistic genius capable of balancing the conflicting elements of the human psyche. Concentrating on the author's final years, Geismar shows Twain enduring the heaviest emotional strains while at the same time artistically and prophetically exposing societal ills.

61. Gerber, John C. *Mark Twain.* Boston: Twayne Publishers, 1988.

Like other books in *Twayne's United States Authors Series,* this one provides a competent introduction for the general reader. Gerber historically situates Twain and his works in his introduction before chronologically accounting for both. The facts are reliable, and Gerber's portrait of Twain draws upon the most important and recent biographical studies available at the time he wrote it. Notes, references, and bibliography direct readers toward more substantial works.

62. Gordon, Edwin. *Mark Twain.* New York: Crowell-Collier Press, 1966.

This book is organized around Twain's occupations and interests, from his early years in the printshop to his later preoccupations with the business world. Gordon mixes fact and fiction and intermingles real and imaginary events in this chronological account, which is directed toward a teenage audience. Gordon concludes his story of Twain's life with the author's business failures in the 1890s. Few dates are supplied and no documentation is offered.

63. Grant, Douglas. *Twain.* Edinburgh, Scotland: Oliver and Boyd, 1962.

Grant makes free use of a substantial amount of Twain's letters in this book, which gives a general sense of Twain's life and career rather than a detailed account. The book is divided into three sections. "S-t-e-a-m Boat A-Comin'!" covers the years 1835–1866; "The Gigantic Picnic" offers a portrait of the good years, 1866–

1889; and "Asking for a Light" ranges over the final years, concluding with a final image of Twain as a failing idealist.

64. Hargrove, Jim. *Mark Twain: The Story of Samuel Clemens.* Chicago: Children's Press, 1984.

    Although this book is a general introduction to Twain's life for young readers, it nonetheless includes a large amount of detail. As might be expected when writing for a young audience, Hargrove structures his narrative around Twain's early years in Hannibal, his experiences as a printer, and his adventures as a steamboat pilot. Hargrove only glances at Twain's middle years and ignores the last decade of the author's life.

65. Hassler, Kenneth. *Mark Twain: Dean of American Humorists.* Charlottesville, N.Y.: SamHar Press, 1975.

    For those just beginning to discover Mark Twain, this brief account of only twenty-eight pages may serve as an informative guide into more lengthy and detailed biographies. In its praise of the author, the booklet builds a one-sided image of a nearly perfect humorist.

66. Henderson, Archibald. *Mark Twain.* London: Duckworth and Company, 1911.

    While not a close friend of Twain's, Henderson was personally acquainted with the author. This study builds upon that personal knowledge and provides significant insight into Twain's life and his works. Henderson sets the direction for many of the biographies that would follow his own, especially in his chapter on "Philosopher, Moralist, Sociologist." Similar concerns over Twain's wide-ranging intellect still provoke critics and scholars. In a fifteen-page bibliography, Henderson provides one of the earliest lists of the articles and reviews accumulating around the subject of Mark Twain.

67. Hill, Hamlin. *Mark Twain: God's Fool.* New York: Harper and Row, 1973.

    A closely detailed account of the last decade of Twain's life, opening with the author's return to the United States in October 1900, after a nearly ten-year sojourn abroad. Relying heavily upon a mass of unpublished material, Hill substantially documents his story of Twain's last years as a "ceaselessly unhumorous existence." Hill portrays a gradually declining Twain, a man driven by unwarranted fears and lingering guilt. At the same time, he exposes the circumstances surrounding the author's family, business, and literary troubles. Hill's book stands as one of the more probing investigations into Twain's later years and into the complicated affairs of a seemingly troubled household. Hill includes a valuable list of source notes for rare manuscript material.

68. Hoffman, Andrew. *Inventing Mark Twain: The Lives of Samuel Langhorne Clemens.* New York: William Morrow and Company, 1997.

Thoroughly researched, this full-length biography springs from Hoffman's impressive knowledge of Twain scholarship and his access to nearly all of Twain's correspondence, notebook entries, unpublished manuscripts, and autobiographical dictations. From this mass of detail, Hoffman reasons and speculates about a Samuel Clemens who created the mask of Mark Twain to hide some fascinating parts of his life. Some of Hoffman's more surprising guesses about the author's secret life, such as possible homosexual behavior, reveal Hoffman's belief that new scholarship requires a different approach and alternative style—so be prepared for a provocative account. Certainly the abundant source material now available has enabled Hoffman to build a biography with much new information. An epilogue briefly traces Twain's fame and the lives of his descendants well into the last part of the twentieth century. Hoffman includes an extensive bibliography and detailed index.

69. Horn, Jason Gary. *Mark Twain and William James: Crafting a Free Self.* Columbia: University of Missouri Press, 1996.

While the humorist from Hannibal and the philosopher from Harvard may seem like an unlikely pairing, Mark Twain and William James did enter into one another's lives during their later years. This book considers their shared interests, while tracing and speculating upon the extent of their relationship. Horn provides a particularly useful discussion of Twain's dream theory and his involvement with the Society for Psychical Research. He underscores Twain's reading of James's work and discusses at length

Twain's comments in the margins of his copy of James's *Varieties of Religious Experience.* The appendixes include previously unpublished material: Twain's 1884 article on "thought-transference" and his only known letters to James.

70. Howard, Oliver, and Goldena Howard. *The Mark Twain Book.* New London, Mo.: Ralls County Book Company, 1985.

This is a brief but densely packed book of facts about Mark Twain. The opening chapters begin by discussing the smallest of details, such as Twain's appearance and clothing. Each chapter progressively enlarges upon major incidents in the author's life, examining, at the same time, Twain's ideas on larger issues such as war, art, religion, and finally death. From the tone of the book, one can tell that the Howards are Twain devotees, but their admiration does not hinder an honest account of their subject. Working from a substantial number of historical documents, plus their own visits and interviews with relatives of those who had firsthand accounts of Twain, the Howards provide an informative handbook for the author's life. They include biographical sketches of family members and numerous photographs documenting different stages in Twain's life.

71. Howells, William Dean. *My Mark Twain: Reminiscences and Criticisms.* New York: Harper and Brothers Publishers, 1910.

Howells's intimate portrait, drawn from his earlier reviews and writings about Mark Twain, offers a penetrating insight into his friend and colleague. His recollections of a forty-year friendship reveal a side of Twain apart from the public image and the often calculated posing of the author. Howells's collection of his reviews, included in the second section of the book, reveal the important role he played in promoting his friend's work and securing Twain's fame.

72. Janssen, Dale H., and Janice J. Beaty. *Mark Twain Walking America Again.* Columbia, Mo.: Dale H. Janssen, 1987.

This is a curious little book that tells about the adventures of Janssen as he toured the country looking like Mark Twain. Attempting to understand Twain from within the author's identity, Janssen, who certainly resembles Twain, begins his trek in Hannibal and tromps around the country in and out of the places Twain visited and called home. As he narrates his experiences, he weaves a biography of sorts with help from more notable biographical and autobiographical sources. Facts are mixed with Janssen's personal experiences and reflections upon Twain's sense of particular events.

73. Kane, Harnett T. *Young Mark Twain and the Mississippi.* New York: Random House, 1966.

Directing her book toward a young audience, Kane provides a reliable and accurate account of Twain's years on the Mississippi River. She relies primarily upon Twain's memories of his boyhood and early adult years as she recounts the important role the Mississippi played in his early life. The narrative begins with young Sam Clemens's fascination with steamboat life and concludes with Clemens the pilot on the Mississippi.

74. Kaplan, Justin. *Mr. Clemens and Mark Twain: A Biography.* New York: Simon and Schuster, 1966.

In 1967, this book won both the National Book Award and the Pulitzer Prize. The work begins with Twain journeying east in 1866 and closely follows the complicated route of Twain's public and private affairs. Kaplan meticulously synthesizes the smallest of details into his portrait of an author divided by the demands of his literary performance and gilded lifestyle and those of a more private and inwardly sensitive writer. Kaplan makes thorough use of available critical and scholarly sources and various collections of Twain's published and unpublished material as he gives an especially detailed account of Twain's last two decades.

75. Kaplan, Justin. *Mark Twain and His World.* New York: Simon and Schuster, 1974.

This illustrated history of Twain's life and times offers only brief summaries and general comments on his major works. It is partially adapted from Kaplan's *Mr. Clemens and Mark Twain,* though not as critically dense in its analysis of Twain's moods and complex personality.

76. Lauber, John. *The Making of Mark Twain: A Biography.* New York: American Heritage Press, 1985.

This work carries the reader from Twain's birth to his courtship and marriage to Olivia Langdon. Lauber presents a direct and factual account of this period while making only occasional forays into interpretation and commentary. The facts are solid, and Lauber's record of them makes for a crisp narrative and a densely packed source of biographical matter.

77. Lawton, Mary. *A Lifetime with Mark Twain: The Memories of Katy Leary, for Thirty Years His Faithful and Devoted Servant.* New York: Harcourt, Brace and Company, 1925.

From 1880 until 1910, Katy Leary was a part of Twain's household. She traveled with the family, attended to its domestic needs, witnessed its prosperity and financial demise, cared for its sick and dying, and remained loyal to it and Twain until the author's death. Leary's memories, as Lawton relates them from interviews with Leary, allow readers to intimately see Twain and his family going about their daily affairs—eating, sleeping, dressing, playing, feuding, and fighting. Some may find the book's folksy and often chatty tone bothersome; nonetheless, it provides an insider's view of Twain as father and husband. Includes photographs of Twain and his family, several of the houses they called home, and their friends and acquaintances.

78. Leacock, Stephen. *Mark Twain.* London: Peter Davies, 1932.

This brief but complete biography offers a mixture of facts, interpretation, and Leacock's own wit, humor, and sarcasm. Leacock is highly supportive of Twain and his work, both of which he determinedly defends as he describes the major events in the author's life.

79. Leary, Lewis. *Mark Twain.* Minneapolis: University of Minnesota Press, 1960.

Leary brings his considerable knowledge about Twain and American literature in general to this publication in the *University of Minnesota Pamphlets on American Writers* series. He offers a general introduction to the life and works of Mark Twain that reviews the major periods and events in the author's life. Leary presents both the comic and serious sides of the writer.

80. Mason, Miriam E. *Mark Twain: Boy of Old Missouri.* Illustrated by Paul Laune. Indianapolis: The Bobbs-Merrill Company, 1942, 1962.

Written for the *Childhood of Famous Americans Series,* this book clearly targets preteens as its audience. It tells the story of young "Sammy" and his many adventures with the Hannibal "gang." It includes illustrations and other appropriate textual apparatus, such as research topics and study questions, for young scholars.

81. Masters, Edgar Lee. *Mark Twain: A Portrait.* New York: Charles Scribner's Sons, 1938.

The facts in this study are reliable though selectively chosen to defend Masters's view of Twain as only a potential comic genius. He avoids presenting Twain as a genuinely great writer, portraying him rather as the creator of near masterpieces. For Masters, Twain squandered his literary talent for the satiric exposure of social ills by ultimately becoming too involved in his own gilded and anxiety-laden lifestyle.

82. McKown, Robin. *Mark Twain: Novelist, Humorist, Satirist, Grassroots Historian, and America's Unpaid Goodwill Ambassador at Large.* New York: McGraw-Hill Book Company, 1974.

Directed toward a general readership and written as an introduction rather than a detailed biography, this full-length narrative of Twain's life briskly strings together the major events in the author's life. McKown offers few dates within his narrative and no documentation of his depiction of events. Some of the facts are wrong and others are highly debatable. McKown lists Twain's books in his concluding section but, oddly enough, leaves out *Adventures of Huckleberry Finn,* a book he mentions only briefly in the text proper.

83. McNeer, May. *America's Mark Twain.* Boston: Houghton Mifflin Company, 1962.

Relying on the work of both Mark Twain and Albert Bigelow Paine, McNeer develops a biography for adolescents. Illustrations and short accounts of Twain's work provocatively set the author in the context of his times.

84. Macnaughton, William R. *Mark Twain's Last Years as a Writer.* Columbia: University of Missouri Press, 1979.

In an attempt to counter a prevailing picture of the late Twain as depressed, obsessed, and creatively stagnant (so persuasively drawn by Justin Kaplan and Hamlin Hill), this book concentrates on the last fifteen years of Twain's life and the author's ability to sustain his creative energy and powers as thinker and writer. Macnaughton devotes over half the book to Twain's life following his daughter Susy's death and his return to the United States in 1900. Keeping Twain at the forefront, Macnaughton draws on events that influenced, distracted, and rearranged Twain's thoughts while he attempted to complete numerous manuscripts.

85. Meltzer, Milton. *Mark Twain: A Writer's Life.* New York: Franklin Watts, 1985.

This book for young readers provides a survey of Twain's life organized around his occupations and major works. It is a fast-paced account but a competent, detailed, and, at times, humorous one. Meltzer only briefly discusses Twain's late years. There is no documentation, but Meltzer includes a helpful bibliographic essay.

86. Messent, Peter. *Mark Twain.* New York: St. Martin's Press, 1997.

As part of the *Modern Novelists* series, this book is primarily intended to introduce readers to Mark Twain's fiction. Messent does offer some basic information on Twain in relation to his work and time, however, along with his critical assessments of Twain's novels. Includes a select list of Twain's major works and secondary criticism.

87. Miers, Earl Schenck. *Mark Twain on the Mississippi.* New York: World Publishing Company, 1957.

This work provides a fictional rendering of Twain's boyhood days in Hannibal and on the Mississippi River. Written for young readers, this biographical tale concludes with Sam Clemens coming of age as Mark Twain, steamboat pilot. A postscript is included that separates "fact from fancy."

88. Miller, Keith. *Mark Twain.* New York: Frederick Ungar Publishing Company, 1983.

This addition to the *Literature and Life* series serves as an introduction to Mark Twain and his major works. As an introductory text, it is not as comprehensive as similar books and offsets its presentation of the facts with a good amount of evaluation and interpretation.

89. Paine, Albert Bigelow. *The Boys' Life of Mark Twain: The Story of a Man Who Made the World Laugh and Love Him. With Many Anecdotes, Letters, Illustrations, etc.* New York: Harper and Brothers Publishers, 1915.

Like Paine's official biography of Twain, this volume is crammed with details about the author's life. The tone is different from the earlier multivolume biography, however, and puts a positive thrust on Twain's actions. Here Paine offers more of a success story as he paints Twain as a model for youth. And unlike his earlier story of the author's life, which disproportionately represents Twain's late years, this version concentrates more on Twain's adventures before his final hardships.

90. Paine, Albert Bigelow. *Mark Twain, a Biography: The Personal and Literary Life of Samuel Langhorne Clemens.* 4 vols. New York: Harper and Brothers Publishers, 1912.

Paine's biography is the standard work for anyone embarking upon a study of Twain's life and career. As a friend of Twain's—the two first met in 1901—Paine was able to collect his information from the author and his family and friends. Paine attempts to provide a complete life study, although his biography is uneven and heavily weighted with details from Twain's later years. His close and intimate accounting of these years remains invaluable, as does his recording of an ample amount of Twain's letters and journal entries. Paine provides no systematic dating of events, so although his biography is chronologically ordered, be prepared to seek out and develop plausible time schemes. Later biographical studies point to some inaccuracies in Paine's work, mostly in the dating of events, yet his multivolume biography remains a crucial document for students and scholars alike.

91. Paine, Albert Bigelow. *A Short Life of Mark Twain.* New York: Harper and Brothers Publishers, 1920.

In this book, Paine condenses information gleaned from his multivolume biography. He uses the same chronological ordering for his narrative of Twain's life but refers far less to the author's letters, journal entries, and other supporting material for documentation.

92. Platt, Mary, and Michael Robinson, compilers. *Mark Twain: An American Voice to the World.* Kennesaw, Ga.: KSC Office of College Relations, 1996.

This catalog contains a list of the items that were displayed at Kennesaw State College in the summer of 1996. The exhibit was developed to celebrate the hundredth anniversary of the culmination of Twain's world lecture tour. On display were first editions and international editions of Twain's works, letters, manuscripts, photographs, and other memorabilia, all selected from various collections. A chronology accompanies the item list, integrating the display into Twain's life and career, and the compilers offer detailed commentaries for many of the 198 items.

93. Press, Skip. *The Importance of Mark Twain.* San Diego, Calif.: Lucent Books, 1994.

This book is part of *The Importance of Biography* series, which is a project designed to give essential information on "individuals who have made a unique contribution to history" in general. Other books in this series cover the lives of people such as Cleopatra, Galileo, Jefferson, Margaret Mead, Richard Nixon, and Jackie Robinson. Each volume acknowledges the unique individual's contribution for a particular time and for ages to come. Although this series appears to be aimed primarily at young adults, Mark Twain's volume includes and evaluates the most recent scholarship on him and supplies substantial documentation in the form of photographs, bibliographies, chronologies, and a comprehensive index.

94. Proudfit, Isabel. *River-Boy: The Story of Mark Twain.* New York: Julian Messner, 1940.

A briskly moving narrative written for young readers, Proudfit's book sparkles with lively quotations from primary and secondary sources. She presents an adventurous and youthful portrait of Twain, concentrating on his life before his move to Hartford, Connecticut. Proudfit does not document her various sources, though she does provide a brief bibliography.

95. Quackenbush, Robert. *Mark Twain? What Kind of Name Is That?: A Story of Samuel Langhorne Clemens.* New York: Prentice-Hall Books for Young Readers, 1984.

Aimed at young readers and emphasizing adventures, this book provides a short and candid introduction to Twain's checkered life. It is delightfully illustrated with a running narrative delivered by a group of comic cats.

96. Sanborn, Margaret. *Mark Twain: The Bachelor Years: A Biography.* New York: Doubleday, 1990.

Sanborn extends the boundaries of traditional research in this biography by physically traveling in Twain's footsteps, which includes speaking to relatives of the author's deceased friends. In order to gain a sense of Twain's experiences as a young man, she examines Twain's early career as a journalist; his riverboat piloting days; his stints as a Confederate volunteer, Nevada silver miner, and far-western journalist; and his becoming a popular lecturer and finally a famed author. The study closes with Twain's marriage in 1870 at the age of thirty-four. Sanborn makes extensive use of letters Twain sent to his family and Olivia Langdon, primarily those housed in the Mark Twain Papers at the Bancroft Library, and includes little-known sources and generally overlooked material in her biography.

97. Sanderlin, George. *Mark Twain: As Others Saw Him.* New York: McGann and Geoghegan, 1978.

Relying heavily upon Twain's own words in the form of abridged quotations, Sanderlin uses the first section of this work to review the facts about the author's life. In section two, he topically organizes Twain's brief opinions on a variety of subjects. In section three, he more directly attends to the project at hand by drawing on newspapers, magazines, journals, and books for a collection of opinions on Twain and his work.

98. Wagenknecht, Edward. *Mark Twain: The Man and His Work.* 3d ed. Norman: University of Oklahoma Press, 1967.

First published in 1935, this book was thoroughly revised by Wagenknecht and published again in 1961. The 1967 edition includes a thirty-page update on Twain criticism and scholarship. Wagenknecht's final version builds upon an abundance of new scholarship, which is thoroughly documented in an impressive bibliography. This "psychograph," as Wagenknecht calls it, accounts for Twain's feelings, attitudes, and intellectual development in relation to the multiple events that completed—and complicated—his life.

99. Walker, I. M. *Mark Twain.* New York: Humanities Press, 1970.

As an introduction for students and general readers, this book offers basic facts and a summary of major events in Mark Twain's life. It also contains selections from some of Twain's major works with pertinent critical commentary. A substantial reference list is included as is a descriptive list of resources for the study of Twain biography.

100. Wector, Dixon. *Sam Clemens of Hannibal.* Boston: Houghton Mifflin Company, 1952.

This book was written as the first of a multivolume definitive biography, a project cut short by Wector's death. This initial volume, however, competently stands alone in its thorough treatment of Twain's early years. Wector offers an in-depth description of the young Sam Clemens and the social, cultural, religious, and political life of Hannibal, Missouri, Twain's boyhood home. He thoroughly documents his sources with extensive footnotes and provides a complete listing of relevant published and unpublished material.

101. Welland, Dennis. *The Life and Times of Mark Twain.* New York: Crescent Books, 1991.

In this oversized book, Welland integrates photographs with a documented and scholarly account of Twain's life and career. The illustrations enlarge our picture of Twain and his times as Welland discusses the author's works. While discussing fingerprinting, palmistry, and *Pudd'nhead Wilson,* for instance, Welland supplies photographs of Twain's palm; he includes photographs of an aging

Harriet Beecher Stowe in a discussion of Nook Farm, where she and Twain were neighbors; and he includes recent scenes from film versions of *Huckleberry Finn* while discussing passages from the book. With its rare and unusual photographs and substantial bits of information, this book enlivens the story of Mark Twain.

102. Welland, Dennis. *Mark Twain in England.* Atlantic Highlands, N.J.: Humanities Press, 1978.

Welland's book details Twain's special relationship with British readers and publishers. This account of Twain's reception and publication in England is built around Twain's correspondence with British friends and, in particular, his close association with Chatto and Windus, his primary British publisher. Much of this material is published for the first time. A valuable index lists a calendar of letters, referenced from the text, which identifies the letter date, recipient, and current owner.

103. Wheeler, Jill C. *Mark Twain.* Minneapolis: Abdo and Daughters, 1996.

Written as a tribute to the young at heart, this book captures a fun-loving Twain for young readers, with upbeat narrative glances at major events in Twain's life. It includes a few choice photographs.

104. Wood, James Playsted. *Spunkwater, Spunkwater! A Life of Mark Twain.* New York: Pantheon Books, 1968.

This is an entertaining illustrated book aimed at young readers or those just encountering Mark Twain. As an introduction to the author's life, it is a reliable and enjoyable book.

# 4

# Critical Biographical Studies

*Twain's was a full, rich, and often complex and contradictory life. The critical studies devoted to it can be the same, though some are richer, some more complex, and some more complete than others. The sources that follow focus either on significant segments of Twain's life, with a critical eye toward understanding his work within these periods, or on his life and work within a particular historical, political, or intellectual context.*

## PERIOD STUDIES

105. Anderson, Kenneth R. *Nook Farm: Mark Twain's Hartford Circle.* Cambridge: Harvard University Press, 1950.

From 1871 to 1891, Mark Twain called Hartford, Connecticut, his home. Some of his most productive years as a writer were spent within a small circle of friends and acquaintances at Nook Farm. This book relates Twain's life within that political, religious, and philosophical environment. It provides biographical material on some of Nook Farm's most famous residents and examines the author's relations with Charles Dudley Warner, Harriet Beecher Stowe, and Joseph Hopkins Twichell in particular. Includes photographs of Twain's neighbors and some of his closest friends. The appendix includes a suppressed chapter from *The Prince and the Pauper,* a substantial note section, and an extensive bibliography.

106. Benson, Ivan. *Mark Twain's Western Years: Together with Hitherto Unreprinted Clemens Western Items.* Stanford, Calif.: Stanford University Press, 1938.

Focusing on Twain's literary development during his Nevada and California years (between 1861 and 1866), Benson provides a detailed account of what he suggests is the crucial formative period in Twain's life as a writer. This study is especially useful for understanding Twain's personal and professional relationships as a journalist for the *Territorial Enterprise,* where he worked for two years, and underscores the influence of fellow journalists on his style and artistic growth. Includes an extensive bibliography of Twain's published writings in Nevada and California newspapers and magazines.

107. Blair, Walter. *Mark Twain and Huck Finn.* Berkeley and Los Angeles: University of California Press, 1960.

Concentrating on Twain's Hannibal and steamboat piloting years, Blair provides a literary and historical account of the forces that influenced the author's composing process. He establishes direct links between the people and ideas that found their way into Twain's life and into his *Adventures of Huckleberry Finn,* in particular. In the final chapters, Blair usefully traces the publication life of the book itself.

108. Branch, Edgar Marquess. *The Literary Apprenticeship of Mark Twain. With Selections from His Apprentice Writings.* Urbana: University of Illinois Press, 1950.

Edgar Marquess Branch divides his book into sections that correspond to Twain's careers as a young man, concentrating on his work as a printer and steamboat pilot, western journalist, and Hawaiian correspondent. Branch treats Twain's early writings in detail as he describes their lasting effect on his art and attitudes, particularly upon his later realism and disillusionment, and he meticulously renders the people, places, and events that were important in shaping the person we know as Mark Twain. Branch includes twenty selections from Twain's early pieces, written between 1852 and 1867.

109. Branch, Edgar M., editor. *Clemens of the* Call: *Mark Twain in San Francisco.* Berkeley and Los Angeles: University of California Press, 1969.

Mark Twain was a reporter for the *San Francisco Daily Morning Call* for four months in 1864, and this book contains a selection of the 198 reports that Twain wrote for the California newspaper. Edgar Branch supplies a commentary for each report that explains the topics Twain addresses, such as earthquakes, opium smugglers, bigamists, Chinese Americans, and, of course, politics. The topical organization of the reports helps organize Twain's various and changing attitudes and interests. Includes a chronological list of Twain's reports and his early dispatches to the *Morning Call* while he was still in Virginia City, Nevada, in 1863.

110. Cardwell, Guy A. *Twins of Genius.* East Lansing: Michigan State College Press, 1953.

Cardwell's book highlights the relationship between Mark Twain and George W. Cable during the years of their closest contact, between 1881 and 1885. Cardwell includes letters the two men wrote to one another during these years and others written through 1906, eighteen of Twain's and twenty of Cable's. He also provides an in-depth account of the joint lecture tour of 1884–1885, which found Twain and Cable sharing the speaker's platform throughout New England and the Midwest, and into Canada. Cardwell provides biographically informative endnotes and a chronological list of letters between Twain and Cable.

111. Clemens, Cyril. *Young Sam Clemens.* Portland, Maine: Leon Tebbetts Editions, 1942.

Cyril Clemens, a distant cousin of Twain's, leads the reader from Twain's birth through his thirty-first year, when the well-known journalist and popular lecturer took his leave of San Francisco and the West. Providing more of an overview than a detailed biography, Clemens scans Twain's childhood days, his work as a printer, and his life on the Mississippi. He focuses more, however, on Twain's western experiences as a miner and journalist. Clemens includes dozens of Twain's newspaper pieces, but there is no source documentation.

112. Clemens, Susy. *Papa: An Intimate Biography of Mark Twain. With a Foreword and Copious Comments by Her Father. Edited with an Introduction by Charles Neider.* New York: Doubleday and Company, 1985.

Although sections of Susy Clemens's recollections of her father, which she started writing when she was thirteen and he was fifty, were published previously, Neider is the first to offer them in their entirety. Primarily written in 1885 and 1886, Susy's biography touchingly portrays Twain as father and family man. Twain's "copious comments," though overshadowing Susy's observations at times, reveal as much about him as a father as they do about the context and matter of his daughter's narrative. Susy is a "frank biographer and an honest one," as Twain notes, and at times, with childlike candor, she depicts her father's vices as well as his virtues. Neider's introduction usefully adds to this portrait as a whole by exploring the curious relationship that continued to develop between father and daughter until the time of Susy's death in 1896.

113. Dolmetsch, Carl. *Our Famous Guest: Mark Twain in Vienna.* Athens: University of Georgia Press, 1992.

"The truth is there remain gaps in our knowledge of Samuel Langhorne Clemens," as Dolmetsch points out, "and especially in the literary biography of 'Mark Twain.'" His book fills some of these as it increases our understanding of both Samuel Clemens the man and Mark Twain the literary artist. Dolmetsch reviews Twain's years abroad from 1891 to 1897, then concentrates on his lengthy stay in Vienna, from September 1897 until May 1899. Using Viennese newspaper items and Twain's journals and writings, Dolmetsch documents Twain's involvement with political and literary activities and his associations with some of Vienna's artists and intellectuals. Dolmetsch joins his analysis of Twain's later years in Vienna with readings of the works that were either started or finished during the author's Vienna sojourn. Overall, Dolmetsch's investigation of Twain's Vienna years challenges a long-held assumption that Twain's life was on the decline between 1890 and the time of his death. This book reveals that he was artistically alive and mentally well.

114. Duckett, Margaret. *Mark Twain and Bret Harte.* Norman: University of Oklahoma Press, 1994.

This book asks its readers to reconsider the life and career of Bret Harte and Twain's role in denying both their proper due. Duckett aims to supply the truth about the relationship between Twain and Harte, which survived in some form from 1864 until Harte's death. She focuses primarily on the literary influence each author had on the other, collaborative projects such as *Ah! Sin,* and Twain's ambivalent acceptance of Harte's work. Duckett's conclusions reflect her thorough research of documents surrounding their relationship, which includes each author's annotated texts of the other's works. Duckett's collection of sources suggests that Twain was not entirely fair in his condemnation of Bret Harte.

115. Fatout, Paul. *Mark Twain in Virginia City.* Bloomington: Indiana University Press, 1964.

Believing that journalistic work helped to define Twain's character, Fatout sets out in this study to reconstruct the period when Mark Twain served as a reporter for the *Territorial Enterprise,* between September 1862 and May 1864. Twain only partly portrays his time at the *Enterprise* in *Roughing It;* Fatout fills many of the gaps in that portrait using reprinted material gathered from the files of Nevada and California newspapers, primarily stories and lost articles of Twain's copied from the *Enterprise.*

116. Gillis, William R. *Gold Rush Days with Mark Twain.* Introduction by Cyril Clemens. New York: Albert and Charles Boni, 1930.

Gillis and Mark Twain became friends and mining partners after meeting in California, at Angel's Camp. While Gillis would remain in Calaveras County for the rest of his life, Twain would leave and profit from his experiences with Gillis and others in the region. While Twain remains the focal point in this book of memoirs, it is about Gillis and the other miners as well. Echoing the language of Twain's *Roughing It,* it describes many of the now-famous events of Twain's mining days and the antics of a rowdy company of men. This work first appeared in 1924 as *Memories of Mark Twain and Steve Gillis.*

117. Harnsberger, Caroline Thomas. *Mark Twain, Family Man.* New York: Citadel Press, 1960.

In this study, Harnsberger narrates the family life of the Clemenses beginning with the 1874 birth of Clara Clemens and continuing until Twain's death and Clara's experiences immediately following that event. Harnsberger met Clara Clemens and relies upon her account of family life, along with that of other family members, for her facts and information. She also uses previously unpublished sections of Twain's "Children's Record," the author's notes on his children's words and deeds, for her portrait of Twain at home. Harnsberger includes some rarely published photographs of the Clemens family.

118. Harris, Susan. *The Courtship of Olivia Langdon and Mark Twain.* New York: Cambridge University Press, 1996.

Harris generally directs her study toward Twain's interaction with the Langdon household and with Olivia Langdon in particular. What results is a broad treatment of Twain's affairs with the Langdon household and an in-depth study of Olivia Langdon herself. Harris makes use of the full set of courtship letters and diaries as well as numerous historical documents. Though only indirectly a biography of Twain, Harris's book reveals his early perspectives on women, marriage, and domesticity. Coverage concludes with Mark Twain and Olivia Langdon settling into their Victorian position as the "Clemenses" in 1873.

119. Hill, Hamlin. *Mark Twain and Elisha Bliss.* Columbia: University of Missouri Press, 1964.

Hill overlooks little in this study as he carefully attends to Twain's business relations with Elisha Bliss and the American Publishing Company. These relations, Hill believes, were "germinal" to Twain's later career as publisher, businessman, and writer. Hill's study is especially useful for an understanding of Twain's composing process and the book promotion process within the subscription publishing industry, which nurtured the popularity of such books as *The Innocents Abroad* (1869), *The Gilded Age* (1873), and *Adventures of Tom Sawyer* (1876). Appendixes provide a typical guide to subscription sales and a bibliography of American Publishing Company books during the company's best years between 1865 and 1884.

120. Hillyer, Katherine. *Young Reporter Mark Twain in Virginia City.* Sparks, Nev.: Western Printing and Publishing Company, 1964.

Hillyer mixes Twain's recollections of the life and times of Virginia City with her own sensational style and packaging to produce this "racy and rollicking" ninety-two-page booklet. Emphasizing reading excitement rather than accurate information, Hillyer casts Twain as an adventuring rascal. There is no documentation, and the photographs and illustrations included are of questionable origin.

121. Jerome, Robert D., and Herbert A. Wisbey Jr. *Mark Twain in Elmira.* Elmira, N.Y.: Mark Twain Society, 1977.

The influence of Elmira, a small city in upstate New York, on the work and life of Mark Twain cannot be overstated. Twain began his courtship with Olivia Langdon and married her in Elmira, home to the well-respected Langdon family, where all his children were born and most buried, along with he and "Livy," in Woodlawn Cemetery. For nearly twenty years after his marriage on February 2, 1870, Twain and his family made their summer home at Quarry Farm, where the author wrote some of his most significant work, most notably portions of *The Adventures of Tom Sawyer, Adventures of Huckleberry Finn,* and *A Connecticut Yankee in King Arthur's Court.* This biographical study combs lesser-known material from local newspapers and privately owned papers as it presents a historically dense document of Twain's association with Elmira. It includes photographs of Twain and the Langdon family. The appendixes contain intimate recollections of Twain by his nephew Jevis Langdon.

122. Lauber, John. *The Inventions of Mark Twain.* New York: Hill and Wang, 1990.

This study covers Twain's entire life and career, although it concentrates on his middle years and the events surrounding the creation and publication of *Adventures of Huckleberry Finn.* Lauber uses an extensive collection of sources, including Twain's published and unpublished writings, thousands of unpublished letters, unpublished literary fragments, and other material available at the Bancroft Library at the University of California, Berkeley. While Lauber provides no exact documentation, he includes a general chapter-by-chapter guide to sources at the end of the book. The perspective that holds the book together revolves around Twain as the inventor of fictions, including the fiction of "Mark Twain." Lauber does not fall back on the image of two selves at war within the author, however; rather he draws Twain the artist and Clemens the man as "mutually dependent." Both selves emerge in Lauber's book as Mark Twain the consummate creator. This is a highly readable, fair, and balanced treatment.

123. Lennon, Nigey. *Mark Twain in California: The Turbulent California Years of Samuel Clemens.* San Francisco: Chronicle Books, 1982.

Lennon chronicles the life of Samuel Clemens on the Pacific Coast after his journalistic apprenticeship in the Nevada Territory. Short on dates and scholarly apparatus, this book whisks through five years of Samuel Clemens's life. It begins with a short chapter on his Nevada experience in 1861, then briskly takes up, at greater length, his reporter's job for the *Morning Call* in San Francisco. It then concludes with Twain's Sandwich Island lectures in the same city in 1866. Lennon includes an ample amount of photographs and prints of handbills for lecture performances.

124. Lennon, Nigey. *The Sagebrush Bohemian: Mark Twain in California.* New York: Paragon House, 1990.

In this expanded version of *Mark Twain in California,* Lennon offers more background material on Twain's mining days and literary fiascoes as well as a fuller account of his "secret" life, the sexual escapades and suicidal tendencies only partially discussed in the earlier book. This book is more sensational in tone than the earlier version, with a definite bias against traditional Twain scholarship.

125. Leon, Phillip W. *Mark Twain and West Point.* Toronto, Ont.: ECW Press, 1996.

Twain visited West Point on at least ten different occasions between 1876 and 1890. Drawing upon a variety of archival sources from public and private collections, some eyewitness accounts, and documents held by West Point, this study documents Twain's relationship with West Point and numerous cadets. Leon suggests the ways in which this relationship affected Twain's writings and, in the case of *A Connecticut Yankee in King Arthur's Court,* directly influenced the treatment of his literary subject matter. The appendixes include Mark Twain's readings at West Point, his relations with the academy's superintendents, and his correspondence with the school's cadets.

126. Lorch, Fred W. *The Trouble Begins at Eight: Mark Twain's Lecture Tours.* Ames, Iowa: Iowa State University Press, 1968.

This study focuses on Twain's career as lecturer as it traces the influence of lecturing on Twain's life and later work. Lorch argues that lecturing transformed Twain from a Wild West journalist into a popular humorist and respected gentleman. He provides useful and convincing evidence for his claim as he accounts for Twain's earliest desires for lecturing fame and his life and friends in Nevada and California.

127. Neider, Charles, editor. *The Travels of Mark Twain.* New York: Coward-McCann, 1961.

Mark Twain wrote five books that were primarily about his travels. Three of the books were about his trips overseas, *The Innocents Abroad* (1869), *A Tramp Abroad* (1880), and *Following the Equator* (1897); the other two books were about travels on the North American continent, *Roughing It* (1872) and *Life on the Mississippi* (1883). Along with the selections he has chosen from all of these books, Neider provides introductory accounts of Twain's life during the writing and publication of his travel narratives. Neider locates Twain "At Home," in Europe, Asia, Africa, Australia, and in "The Islands."

128. Mack, Effie Mona. *Mark Twain in Nevada.* New York: Charles Scribner's Sons, 1947.

This is the first book to exclusively concentrate on Twain's three years in Nevada, between 1861 and 1864. It is as much a story of the social and political events taking place in Nevada during Twain's stay there as it is a biography. Nonetheless, this is the earliest full-length study of Twain's life to show the formative part the author's western experience played in shaping his literary career. The back matter includes a valuable and lengthy index of names and places connected to Twain's Nevada years.

129. McWilliams, Jim. *Mark Twain in the* St. Louis Post-Dispatch, *1874–1891.* Troy, N.Y.: Whitson Publishing Company, 1997.

This meticulously constructed book provides an unusual type of biographical fare, the life of Mark Twain as told through a substantial collection of newspaper clippings. Taken from what was known at different periods as the *Dispatch,* the *Post,* and the *Post-Dispatch,* the newspaper items represent seventeen years of reports about Twain from contemporaries. As McWilliams explains, the pieces complement existing Twain biographies and his autobiographical material. Gathered here are nearly three hundred pieces—anecdotes, memoirs, articles, stories, and interviews—that provide an "exhaustive record" of Mark Twain's activities. Some of the items record Twain's own writings and sayings, while the longer items were written by his friends and various reporters. The shortest pieces contain mostly gossip and speculation by those preoccupied with Twain's life. Annotations situate the clippings in the context of Twain's life and work and supply further information for understanding material included in each item.

130. Petit, Arthur G. *Mark Twain and the South.* Lexington: University Press of Kentucky, 1974.

This study traces Twain's ambivalent feelings about the South beginning with his early years in the Nevada Territory and on to his last years as a writer. Drawing Twain as a product of reconstruction, his fractured personality a reflection of the southern condition in general, Petit accounts for the author's life as one of shifting allegiances to lost southern principles and newly acquired northern attitudes, conflicting feelings that gradually led to a personal and artistic stagnation. Petit offers an impressive list of sources from public and private collections.

131. Quick, Dorothy. *Enchantment: A Little Girl's Friendship with Mark Twain.* Norman: University of Oklahoma, 1961.

Dorothy Quick was one of a small group of girls that Twain dubbed his "Angelfish," and this account covers the relationship she shared with the author in the last few years of his life. Quick visited Twain in his New York home at Fifth Avenue, at Stormfield, Connecticut, and while he vacationed in Bermuda. Aside from their personal time together, they corresponded with one another until the year of Twain's death in 1910. Some of the letters that passed between them are included in this book.

132. Rodney, Robert M. *Mark Twain Overseas: A Biographical Account of His Voyages, Travels, and Reception in Foreign Lands, 1866–1910.* Washington, D.C.: Three Continents Press, 1993.

This book aims to establish the importance of Mark Twain's travels abroad and his eminent place as American literary ambassador. Twain spent a total of fourteen years abroad, a "large dimension" of the author's experience, which, as this book illustrates, had a lasting impact upon him and those he met in his travels. Each chapter attends to one of Twain's particular excursions: to Hawaii in 1866, England in 1872–1874, across the European continent in 1878–1879, around the world in 1895–1896, at homes abroad between 1896–1900, and in Bermuda during Twain's final years. Includes a valuable appendix section with a list of Twain's friends abroad, his lectures, and various places of residence.

133. Shillingsburg, Miriam Jones. *At Home Abroad: Mark Twain in Australasia.* Jackson: University Press of Mississippi, 1988.

While this work covers only a brief period in Twain's life, his fifteen-week lecture tour in Australia and New Zealand in 1895, it is clear, incisive, and complete. Shillingsburg thoroughly documents an extensive set of facts and quotations beginning with the financial failures that led to Twain's tour, and on through Sydney, Melbourne, Adelaide, the Australian countryside, and then New Zealand. Including ample amounts of letters, notebook entries, journalistic accounts, and interviews with Twain, Shillingsburg expands upon the primary material found in Twain's *More Tramps Abroad* (Chatto and Windus). Shillingsburg includes an extensive index covering names, places, events, and Twain's lecture topics.

134. Steinbrink, Jeffrey. *Getting to Be Mark Twain.* Berkeley and Los Angeles: University of California Press, 1991.

This study treats the period of Twain's life between 1868 and 1871, when Steinbrink suggests that Samuel Clemens essentially assumed the posture of Mark Twain. Steinbrink considers these the formative years for the writer who was beginning to take his place in the dominant culture and who would eventually become one of its most accessible icons. Steinbrink supplies an ample amount of material from primary sources and allows Twain to tell about his formative changes, through a judicious interleaving of the author's letters into his account. Especially useful for understanding Twain's experiences at the *Buffalo Express* and the *Galaxy Magazine.*

135. Taper, Bernard, editor. *Mark Twain's San Francisco.* New York: McGraw-Hill Book Company, 1963.

In this book, Taper gathers the writings Mark Twain published in Nevada and California papers between 1863 and 1866. His introduction offers a general review of Twain's life.

136. Turner, Arlin. *Mark Twain and George W. Cable: The Record of a Literary Friendship.* East Lansing: Michigan State University Press, 1960.

Mark Twain and George Cable toured together as lecturers in 1884–1885. In this book, Turner collects the letters Cable sent to his wife, which taken together provide a nearly daily account of his and Twain's activities during the tour. The letters reveal how Twain managed the strenuous demands of touring often by conversing with Cable for hours after performances; they also reveal the camaraderie Cable and Twain shared and the close relations that existed between Twain and the tour's manager, Major James B. Pond. Turner's commentary supplies the necessary context for the letters. Includes previously unpublished letters from Twain to Major Pond, as well as Cable's speeches at Twain's seventieth birthday dinner and at Twain's memorial service in New York, on November 30, 1910.

137. Wallace, Elizabeth. *Mark Twain and the Happy Island.* Chicago: A. C. McClurg and Company, 1913.

Albert Bigelow Paine provides the introductory note for this book, a collection of the author's fond memories of Mark Twain during his trips to Bermuda. Wallace's firsthand account of the inception of Twain's "Angelfish," a club for young girls, and of Twain's spirited relations with H. H. Rogers while both men enjoyed Bermuda, adds an intimate insight into Twain's final years. Includes Twain's letters to Wallace.

138. Webster, Samuel Charles, editor. *Mark Twain: Business Man.* Boston: Little, Brown and Company, 1946.

Webster wants to clear the name of his father, Charles L. Webster, and "correct Mark Twain's memory" of his dealings with him. He claims that Twain used Charles Webster as a scapegoat for the failings of the publishing house of Charles L. Webster and Company. Working from the many letters Twain wrote to various people during his relations with Charles Webster, and the letters from Twain to "Charley," Samuel Webster shows that his father was Twain's close friend and had worked steadily to successfully build the publishing company. Webster's account redraws the image of Twain as a victim but does not undermine his abilities as a writer. Clara Clemens agreed with Webster and allowed the inclusion of letters that might somewhat tarnish her own father's image.

139. Williams, George, III. *Mark Twain: His Adventures at Aurora and Mono Lake.* Riverside, Calif.: Tree by the River Publishing, 1986.

With this book, Williams concentrates on Twain's short career as a silver miner at Aurora, Nevada, in 1861. For the most part, Williams lets Twain tell his story of a harsh and disappointing experience through his correspondence with his brother and sister, Orion and Pamela. Williams includes Twain's often caustic observations on Mono Lake and the surrounding area.

140. Williams, George, III. *Mark Twain: His Life in Virginia City, Nevada.* Riverside, Calif.: Tree by the River Publishing, 1985.

As with other books in this series, this one provides the general reader with rare and unpublished photographs, as well as a guide to the people Twain knew and the places he frequented—in this case, during the years he lived in Nevada, between July 1861 and May 1864. Williams emphasizes Twain's years as a reporter for the *Enterprise,* building his account around Twain's letters, journals, and newspaper articles as well as personal recollections of the young writer.

141. Williams, George, III. *On the Road with Mark Twain in California and Nevada.* Dayton, Nev.: Tree by the River Publishing, 1994.

A lively tour guide to Mark Twain's travels in California and Nevada. Packaged in a glossy-covered paperback, much like a road atlas, this volume makes no pretensions to scholarly authority, though the dates are accurate and primary material reliable. This volume offers a mix of letters, notes, news articles, and rare photographs of the people Twain knew and the places he stayed while in the West. As part of Williams's *Mark Twain in the West* series, this volume provides a general coverage of Twain's western years as a whole, while other volumes attend to particular parts of Twain's western experience.

142. Willis, Resa. *Mark and Livy: The Love Story of Mark Twain and the Woman Who Almost Tamed Him.* New York: Atheneum Publishers, 1992.

While this book offers a definitive biography of Olivia Langdon Clemens, it also indirectly provides rare insight into an intimate side of her husband. Letters between Twain and Olivia Langdon provide a personal view of Twain's failings and successes, and his appetite for fame and wealth. Olivia Langdon emerges here as an astute editor and strong woman, and Twain as both capable of creating an image of his wife for public consumption and recognizing her prominent place in the most private of his thoughts and emotions.

## CONTEXTUAL STUDIES

143. Baetzhold, Howard G. *Mark Twain and John Bull: The British Connection.* Bloomington: Indiana University Press, 1970.

This study examines Twain's literary and personal relationship with a wide range of British thinkers and writers, who to varying degrees influenced Twain's own thought and work. In particular, Baetzhold discusses Twain's association with the Chattos and Henry M. Stanley, and with writers such as Anthony Trollope, Robert Louis Stevenson, Bram Stoker, and Rudyard Kipling. Baetzhold provides a meticulous record of Twain's visits to England beginning with his 1872 sojourn. He argues that Twain substantially borrowed from British writers, from Milton and Bunyan to Defoe, Swift, and Fielding, and was philosophically influenced by his reading of Carlyle and W. E. H. Lecky. Twain held, according to Baetzhold, ambivalent feelings about American democracy and was deeply attracted to the British system of government. This book includes a thorough index and extensive set of notes.

144. Bridgman, Richard. *Traveling in Mark Twain.* Berkeley and Los Angeles: University of California Press, 1987.

This study traces Twain's travels and examines the author's preoccupation with travel, in both his life and works. It begins by recording Twain's ideas and movements with a consideration of *Innocents Abroad* and *Roughing It.* Bridgman reads both books as exposing Twain's psychic drive toward ever-receding horizons and initiating his search for vanishing truths. The search continues throughout Twain's life, as Bridgman maintains, keeping Twain moving across mental and physical landscapes. The book includes a discussion of the often trying circumstances surrounding the writing and production of Twain's travel books.

145. Budd, Louis J. *Mark Twain: Social Philosopher.* Bloomington: Indiana University Press, 1962.

    Primarily aimed at situating Twain's work within the context of its social, economic, and political background, this study also serves as a narrative of a mind in progress. Although this is not a "psychobiography," Budd shows that we can come to a deeper understanding of Twain through his politics. Twain's knowledge of political life was wide and detailed, but his political sentiments were often inconsistent. Budd clearly maps such changing ideas, tracing them from Twain's journalistic involvement with local politics during his western years to his later and more grand actions on the national and international scene. This book is carefully documented.

146. Camfield, Gregg. *Sentimental Twain: Samuel Clemens in the Maze of Moral Philosophy.* Philadelphia: University of Pennsylvania Press, 1994.

    As a "reconstructive history," this work traces the impact of the "sentimental world-view" on Twain's thought and writings. As a history of ideas and a biography of mind, it represents an attempt to understand Twain's "intellectual quest" for a middle ground between "idealistic sentimentalism" and "materialistic determinism." Camfield offers one of the more thorough explorations of Twain's psychology and its grounding in nineteenth-century intellectual history. He also provides a useful set of discursive notes and a lengthy bibliography of literary and philosophical works.

147. Canby, Henry Seidel. *Turn West, Turn East: Mark Twain and Henry James.* Boston: Houghton Mifflin Company, 1951.

    In this "critical biography," Canby examines the life and work of Mark Twain and Henry James, focusing on what he claims is an American impulse: the pursuit of the "Western experience" and reliance on Europe for "fresh intellectual stimulation." With Twain, Canby concentrates on the westward pursuit. Canby peppers his story of Twain and his family's frontier experience with speculations, often filling in narrative gaps with Twain's own questionable "facts." Canby includes only a partial bibliography; there is no documentation for facts or conjectures.

148. Cardwell, Guy. *The Man Who Was Mark Twain: Images and Ideologies*. New Haven, Conn.: Yale University Press, 1991.

This study considers Twain's life against a set of select topics, with some of the more highly charged subjects being sexuality, pedophilia, and racism. Cardwell wants to understand the man behind the myth, to "clear away a number of conceptual and biographical encumbrances." His biographical housecleaning leaves readers with both a highly talented writer and a man with numerous personality problems. A study of both Twain's inner life and his public image, Cardwell's book disentangles and calls into question the many biographical visions and revisions of Mark Twain.

149. Cox, James M. *Mark Twain: The Fate of Humor.* Princeton, N.J.: Princeton University Press, 1966.

While recognizing the indispensable contributions of Paine, Brooks, and DeVoto, Cox carries Mark Twain studies to yet another level in this book. Cox organizes his biographical matter around Twain as a personality, beginning with the author's adoption of his pseudonym around 1863. The name Mark Twain, according to Cox, provided Samuel Clemens with an artistic venue through which he could discover, reveal, and fulfill himself. Mixing fact and psychological theory, along with primary documents such as letters and autobiographical entries, Cox discloses how Twain reordered his past through his art and constructed his life and career upon that creative act. The book's first chapter is particularly informative in its discussion of Sam Clemens's "discovery" of his pseudonym.

150. Cummings, Sherwood. *Mark Twain and Science: Adventures of a Mind.* Baton Rouge: Louisiana State University Press, 1988.

This book tells the story of Twain's mind as it came to grips with scientific thought in the late nineteenth century. Cummings does more in this book, however, than just trace Twain's relationship to science; he situates Twain's thinking in a wide range of ideas, including the religious, historical, and philosophical debates of his day as well as quickly developing scientific theories. In particular, Cummings links Twain's own developing ideas with those of Darwin, W. E. H. Lecky, and, perhaps most closely, the French intellectual Hippolyte Taine. Cummings establishes Twain's knowledge of these thinkers and traces their ideas into four works: *The Prince and the Pauper, Adventures of Huckleberry Finn, A Connecticut Yankee in King Arthur's Court,* and *Pudd'nhead Wilson.*

151. David, Beverly R. *Mark Twain and His Illustrators: Volume I (1869–1875).* Troy, N.Y.: Whitson Publishing Company, 1986.

In his useful introduction to this book, Alan Gribben points out that as "an illustrated literary comedian," Twain was thoroughly entrenched in the "tradition of multimedia productions." David reveals just how deeply involved Twain was with his illustrators and the sketches they created for his work. In this first volume, she explores this relationship in connection with Twain's early subscription books and publications: *The Innocents Abroad, Mark Twain's (Burlesque) Autobiography, Roughing It, The Gilded Age, Sketches, New and Old,* and *The Adventures of Tom Sawyer.* Each book is covered in a separate chapter which, aside from a well-documented discussion of Twain's relations with publishers and illustrators, includes extensive endnotes and a list of illustrations shown.

152. Doyno, Victor A. *Writing Huck Finn: Mark Twain's Creative Process.* Philadelphia: University of Pennsylvania Press, 1991.

This study moves in two directions toward a single goal: an understanding of Mark Twain's artistic mind. Specifically, Doyno uses Twain's most celebrated novel as a means for exploring Twain's interest in such issues as nobility and individualism, morality and religion, and notions of literacy. Working from the manuscript version of *Huckleberry Finn*—with its many revisions—Doyno shows how Twain's humor, style, and characterizations developed in relation to less literary issues and how his imagination matured while the novel developed, and also examines the relation between Twain's life and art in general.

153. Eble, Kenneth E. *Old Clemens and W. D. H.: The Story of a Remarkable Friendship.* Baton Rouge: Louisiana State University Press, 1985.

Mark Twain and William Dean Howells first met in 1869 in the editor's office at the *Atlantic Monthly.* They would become the closest of literary friends. Working mostly from primary materials—letters, notebook entries, and writings of both men, Eble tells the story of this friendship. He notes the many parallels in their early lives and suggests how a similar background attracted them to one another. "Each influenced the other toward developing his distinctive talents," Eble points out, and as they aged they learned to mutually appreciate one another. This book offers one of the more insightful studies of Twain's character and temperament.

154. Ensor, Allison. *Mark Twain and the Bible.* Lexington: University of Kentucky Press, 1969.

This study draws a picture of a man divided by religious sentiments, a Twain whose work reveals his ambivalent relations with the Bible and its authority. It portrays Twain as a selective reader of the Bible as a whole, though particularly struck by Genesis and its creation story. Ensor reads Twain's letters, journals, and fiction as highly charged with biblical images, but presents the author himself as split between belief and doubt, between a traditional reverence for biblical themes and an irreverent opposition to them.

155. Fingers, Charles J. *Mark Twain, the Philosopher Who Laughed at the World.* Girard, Kans.: Haldeman-Julius Company, 1924.

Fingers believes that few people really read Mark Twain, the author who he claims is more explosive than most know. His booklet is one of the first to consider Twain a powerful thinker, as a "true philosopher with a balanced system" and "coherently complete" set of ideas. Relying heavily upon letters and writings from Twain's later years, Fingers draws Twain as an intensely serious thinker who, with a "strong sense of cosmic humor," fired away at oppression and injustice as he found them. Includes items concerning his friends and acquaintances during his final years.

156. Fisher, Henry W. *Abroad with Mark Twain and Eugene Field: Tales They Told to a Fellow Correspondent.* New York: Nicholas

L. Brown, 1922.

Henry Fisher came to know Twain through intermittent associations with him during his frequent trips abroad. Fisher had met Twain in Chicago in 1879, when both men were early in their careers as journalists, and upon meeting him in Berlin, in 1891, he became the unofficial tour guide for Twain and his family. As Fisher admits, his book does not necessarily provide any ordered pattern but springs from an assorted blend of Twain's words and actions.

157. Fishkin, Shelley Fisher. *Was Huck Black? Mark Twain and African American Voices.* New York: Oxford University Press, 1993.

Although primarily a critical analysis of the *Adventures of Huckleberry Finn* and the place of African American voices in the work, this study asks readers to reexamine Twain's formative years in connection with those influential voices, a context that Fishkin believes "shaped Twain's creative imagination at its core." She provides meticulously documented discursive notes and a thorough index of names and subjects—over a hundred pages of documentation in all.

158. Foner, Philip S. *Mark Twain: Social Critic.* New York: International Publishers Company, 1958.

Foner begins his book with a brief review of Twain's life before he takes up topics that were intricately linked to the author's thought and expression. Politics, religion, capitalism, race issues, and international relations are Foner's primary topics, and he offers a detailed examination of Twain's thinking on each of these, along with information on his more active involvement with his ideas. His discussion of Twain's Freemasonry, Mugwump politics, and anti-imperialist activities are particularly useful. Foner includes a full bibliography of books, manuscripts, and unpublished manuscripts.

159. Frear, Walter Francis. *Mark Twain and Hawaii.* Chicago: Lakeside Press, 1947.

For Frear, Twain's trip to Hawaii stands as a turning point in the author's career, as an "interstice" between the early, rough years of experience and the years in which Twain developed into a successful writer and prominent personality. With this importance in mind,

Frear offers a meticulously documented account of Twain's visit to Hawaii. He presents the facts surrounding Twain's trip with an abundance of detail and copious citations. He offers details about Twain's choice of hotels, the author's many visitors, his trips around the island and to other islands, and his lectures. Includes a substantial section of appendixes that provide further information on Hawaii, and a nearly complete collection of all Twain wrote in connection with Hawaii, for example, letters for the *Sacramento Union* and the *Alta California,* and articles for the *Galaxy.*

160. Fulton, Joe B. *Mark Twain's Ethical Realism: The Aesthetics of Race, Class, and Gender.* Columbia: University of Missouri Press, 1997.

Fulton's book is primarily a study of Twain's style and its implications for his ideas on race, class, and gender issues. He makes full use of the theories of Mikhail Bakhtin, especially "dialogism" and "polyphony," as he attempts to "dispel some myths about Mark Twain's aesthetics." In doing so, he offers provocative insights into Twain's writing habits and methods, taking a literary biographical perspective from which readers can link Twain's style to his ethics. His target texts include *The Prince and the Pauper, Adventures of Huckleberry Finn, A Connecticut Yankee in King Arthur's Court,* and *Pudd'nhead Wilson.* Nearly twenty pages of works cited reveal Fulton's breadth of documentation.

161. Ganzel, Dewey. *Mark Twain Abroad: The Cruise of the* Quaker City. Chicago: University of Chicago Press, 1968.

This work adds to and expands upon *The Innocents Abroad* and its account of Twain's tour of Europe and the Holy Land. After a general introduction to the phenomenon known as the "European Tour" and the complex preparations and multiple problems related to getting the steamship *Quaker City* underway, Ganzel closely considers Twain's activities and the associations and friendships he formed during his five-month excursion abroad. What makes this book biographically useful is Ganzel's attempt to understand Twain's attitudes toward Europe and the Holy Land within the context of the his cultural and religious background. The appendixes include fragments of Twain's unfinished play about his first trip abroad and a *Quaker City* passenger list, which corrects and supplements an earlier one offered by Albert Bigelow Paine.

162. Gibson, William M., editor. *Mark Twain's* Mysterious Stranger *Manuscripts.* Berkeley and Los Angeles: University of California Press, 1969.

From 1897 to 1908, Twain sporadically worked on his tale of a mysterious stranger, revising and altering a changing body of texts in line with many of his own changing moods and experiences. In this book, Gibson presents three different manuscripts in the order and style believed to be nearest Twain's intentions. His introduction, along with nearly two hundred pages of supplementary material, is quite useful for those attempting to understand Twain's later years. In particular, Gibson accounts for the incidents that played a large part in the psychology and philosophy exhibited in Twain's dream tales and the shifting political and religious sentiments exposed in the *Stranger* manuscripts.

163. Gillman, Susan. *Dark Twins: Imposture and Identity in Mark Twain's America.* Chicago: University of Chicago Press, 1989.

This book accounts for Mark Twain and Twain's America as both turned from the nineteenth to the twentieth century. Gillman is mostly concerned with identity shifts, and her book explores the question of what shapes one's sense of self and one's cultural identity. It is a complex exploration but one that locates Twain as an embodiment of his and his country's identity crises. Gillman provides details on Twain's investigations into the mystery of identity and his attempts to resolve conflicts by turning to the available "vocabularies" of his time. Using Twain's letters and notebooks, Gillman provides especially useful information on Twain's knowledge of scientific and psychological theories, many of which played an influencial role in his literary preoccupation with dream tales. This is a highly detailed study that is especially useful for understanding Twain's later years and his involvement with the racial, sexual, biological, and even spiritual controversies about identity that flourished in turn-of-the-century America. Gillman's discursive endnotes deepen and thicken her "literary analysis of cultural history."

164. Griffith, Clark. *Achilles and the Tortoise: Mark Twain's Fictions.* Tuscaloosa: University of Alabama Press, 1998.

Griffith's curiosity sets the direction for this book, which confronts Twain's contradictory attitudes and shifting philosophies. Griffith aims to understand the ever-changing Twain and the ways in which the author organized his fictions, and to what degree he was reorganized by them. He approaches Twain's comic and serious sides in the seven essays that make up his book, considering "The Comic Impulse," "The Creation of Caricatures," "The Twin Faces of Reality," and "Philosophical Speculations about Reality." Griffith concludes by connecting Twain and Melville as "purveyors of essentially the same dark vision."

165. Hays, John Q. *Mark Twain and Religion: A Mirror of American Eclecticism.* Edited by Fred A. Rodewald. New York: Peter Lang Publishing, 1989.

This book points to the multiple influences from various religious systems and ideas on Twain's thinking. In the process, it questions a strong strain of scholarship that portrays Twain's later years as filled with despair and pessimism. Rather, Hays draws Twain as a man of "spiritual integrity," one unwilling to remain permanently in any one frame of mind, in constant search of a satisfying worldview. Twain was certainly exposed to Calvinistic Presbyterianism in his youth, but Jane Clemens, his Presbyterian mother, by no means prescribed a religious path for her son. Clemens was also exposed to the more liberal religious thinking of his father and uncle John Quarles. Hays considers the effects of Deism, Determinism, and Romanticism on Twain's thought and writings as well.

166. Johnson, James L. *Mark Twain and the Limits of Power: Emerson's God in Ruins.* Knoxville: University of Tennessee Press, 1982.

Ralph Waldo Emerson certainly cast an influential shadow over much of nineteenth-century American literature, and in the case of Whitman and Dickinson directly influenced poetic style and subject matter. With Twain, however, Emerson served not so much as a direct influence but more as a companion mind within a particular American stream of thought. Like Emerson, Johnson contends, Twain never wholly lost his fascination with liberated selfhood. Tracing the connecting lines of thought between these two men enables Johnson to alter the general portrait of Twain as an aging, despairing skeptic. Johnson approaches Twain's work, primarily *The Adventures of Tom Sawyer, Adventures of Huckleberry Finn, A Connecticut Yankee,* and *The Mysterious Stranger,* as reflections of the author's own artistic, intellectual, and emotional involvement with the problematic notion of a free and powerful self.

167. Knoper, Randall. *Acting Naturally: Mark Twain in the Culture of Performance.* Berkeley and Los Angeles: University of California Press, 1995.

This book offers a study of both the culture of performance and the effect a performing culture had on Twain's thinking and emotional expression. Performances, from popular entertainments such as minstrel shows to the antics of P. T. Barnum and the theatrics of late-nineteenth-century psychics, shaped Twain's sense of self, as Knoper contends. As his book illustrates, Twain's involvement with popular performances reflected his own explorations of human posturing and, to some degree, conditioned his own sense of identity.

168. Krause, Sydney J. *Mark Twain as Critic.* Baltimore: Johns Hopkins Press, 1967.

"Twain was no boob," as this study clearly shows; this book reappraises his values, thought, convictions, and worldview in an effort to explore the depth and breadth of his intellect. From playing the part of an untutored fool in his early years to donning the "grumbler" mask of his later years, Twain, as Krause points out, was continually the thoughtful critic, commenting on stage and oratorical performances, architecture, poetic and newspaper style, and novelists' techniques. While Krause acknowledges that Twain's critical eye may not have been as sharp as some would like, his study goes a long way toward exploding the "myth that he had no capacity" for insightful analysis.

169. Lynn, Kenneth S. *Mark Twain and Southwestern Humor.* Boston: Little, Brown and Company, 1959.

As its title indicates, this study develops its narrative of Mark Twain within the boundaries of his relation to the tradition of Southwestern humor. Lynn reviews Twain's background as a Southwestern humorist and accounts for his involvement with other humorists in the Southwestern tradition.

170. Michelson, Bruce. *Mark Twain on the Loose: A Comic Writer and the American Self.* Amherst: University of Massachusetts Press, 1995.

In his introduction to this book, Michelson warns that he has "heresies to suggest" about Mark Twain, "as personage, as text, and as myth." His book then convincingly shows that Mark Twain escaped and continues to escape definition. Michelson nonetheless aims at some loose understanding of Twain's identity. The central concerns in Twain's life and work, as Michelson emphasizes, revolve around escaping all that threatens to limit a free, even disruptive, development. Michelson's psychological portrait reveals further that Twain's life, like his work, refuses to be contained by critics, retaining its sense of mystery through a complex maze of twists, turns, and surprises that subverts an overly serious approach to it. This resistance to "categories and boundaries" is an essential part of Twain's personality, as Michelson suggests, and the necessary force driving an evolving self and a disruptive humor. Michelson includes a substantial set of discursive notes.

171. Norton, Charles A. *Writing Tom Sawyer: The Adventures of a Classic.* Jefferson, N.C.: McFarland and Company, Publishers, 1983.

This book directs itself toward the crafting of *The Adventures of Tom Sawyer* and to the events that surrounded Twain's writing of this novel. In part 1, Norton meticulously details Twain's experiences beginning with the book's "aborted" starts in 1872 and 1873, through trying moments of creative activity in 1874 and 1875, production and publication problems in 1875 and 1876, and finally to a type of literary postpartum depression in 1876. Part 2 establishes the circumstances surrounding Twain's initial step toward "respectable" authorship and the immediate literary and historical background. Norton focuses on the critical fate of *Tom Sawyer* in the last two parts of his study. As literary biography, this book provides a wealth of detail within a limited range of subject matter.

172. Pellowe, William C. S. *Mark Twain: Pilgrim from Hannibal.* New York: Hobson Book Press, 1945.

This book suggestively draws a portrait of Twain's inner life and "Twain the man" by tracing his personality development through his association with religious ideas. It covers the whole of Twain's life from a limited, though important, perspective, tracing his evolving mental and spiritual growth through an early Presbyterian upbringing, through the possible influence of more liberal-minded ministers, and on to a later skepticism and pessimism. In particular, the book focuses on Joseph Twichell and the Beecher family as two major influences.

173. Quirk, Tom. *Mark Twain: A Study of the Short Fiction.* New York: Twayne Publishers, 1997.

In this sixty-sixth volume of *Twayne's Studies in Short Fiction,* Quirk discusses the life of Mark Twain in relation to the crafting and production of his short fiction. Quirk divides his book into three parts, devoting the first part to a detailed review of Twain's entire life. He discusses Twain's early years, between 1863 and 1873, in relation to his career as journalist and literary comedian; his middle years, from 1874 to 1890, as creatively charged; and his later years as psychologically dampened, though not artistically flattened, by the weight of circumstance. In the second part of the book, Quirk allows Twain to speak for himself through a selection of his essays that focus on his own working principles as a writer. In the last section, Quirk gathers a selection of criticism that addresses Twain's artistry and compositional techniques, including pieces by William Dean Howells, Louis Budd, Don Florence, Walter Blair, and Gregg Camfield. Includes a chronology and a selected bibliography of primary and secondary works.

174. Regan, Robert. *Unpromising Heroes: Mark Twain and His Characters.* Berkeley and Los Angeles: University of California Press, 1966.

Often in the folktale tradition, a youth with little chance of succeeding in life still does just that—succeeds. Such a youth represents the "unpromising hero" for Regan. In this book, he explores the relationship that exists between the folktale tradition of unpromising heroes and Mark Twain's sensibilities and emotional growth. This image of a hapless hero informs the growth of some of Twain's most recognizable characters (Tom Sawyer, Hank Morgan, and Pudd'nhead, for instance), and Regan accounts for its importance in the development of Sam Clemens's alter ego, Mark Twain. The book moves in two directions as Regan examines Twain's writings and the "shadowy recesses of his inner life from which the writings issued." Regan provides a substantial amount of documentation for this book's blend of fact, speculation, and interpretation.

175. Schirer, Thomas. *Mark Twain and the Theatre.* Nürnberg: Hans Carl, 1984.

In its attempt to dispel the notion that Twain had little interest in the theater, this book mines a little-developed biographical vein. It explores the extent of Twain's involvement with the theater—at times intense—and establishes the degree to which drama and theatrics informed his creative process. Schirer pinpoints the specific events of Twain's life that establish his close connection to the theater, revealing Twain's knowledge of the theater through his letters and his associations with actors, producers, and financial backers. Schirer examines Twain's complex relations to his own work and the possibility of dramatizing it, as well as the collaborations and negotiations on plays with Bret Harte and William Dean Howells. In all, Twain was involved in ten dramatic collaborations, translated three plays from German to English, authorized the dramatic rendering of seven of his novels, and began eleven dramatizations himself, five of which were completed as prose works.

176. Scott, Arthur L. *On the Poetry of Mark Twain: With Selections from His Verse.* Urbana: University of Illinois Press, 1966.

Scott does not intend to convince his readers that Twain had a talent for poetry; rather, he challenges the assumption that he detested it. Scott, in fact, claims that from "his boyhood until his death," Twain enjoyed reading, hearing, and producing poetry. In his lengthy introduction, Scott documents Twain's attraction to poetry. He begins with Twain's poetic experiments as a schoolboy, discusses the strange poetic combinations he sent in his later letters home, describes the rhyming parodies he published during his western years, and traces his poetic attempts at light verse to his early years at Hartford. At the same time, Scott establishes Twain's more serious involvement with the poetry of Browning and Omar Khayyám and discusses his continuing engagement with the writing and reading of poetry. Scott includes dozens of Twain's poems.

177. Seelye, John. *Mark Twain in the Movies: A Meditation with Pictures.* New York: Viking Press, 1977.

This is not a study of Twain and his appearances on film but rather a "meditation" on the meaning of Twain's image for image-conscious people. In sixteen short chapters, Seelye presents Twain's various sides or poses as represented in some of the more memorable photographs of him. Seelye juxtaposes select biographical material against the dominant images projected by these photographs in an effort to create a counterimage, one that allows for a more complex portrait, an understanding of Twain outside the well-constructed snapshots. This book includes some rarely seen photographs that belonged to Isabel V. Lyon, Twain's secretary from 1902 to 1909.

178. Skandera-Trombley, Laura E. *Mark Twain in the Company of Women.* Philadelphia: University of Pennsylvania Press, 1994.

Beginning her study with the claim that biographers have generally ignored the place of women in Twain's life, Skandera-Trombley sets off to remedy this neglect in her account of Twain's relations with influential women. Chief among these was Olivia Langdon, whose image (as a controlling wife and censorious editor) Skandera-Trombley reshapes, making her an active participant in Twain's literary production. This study also establishes Twain's personal and intellectual ties to many other women, some as different as Mary Fairbanks, Isabella Beecher Hooker, and Isabel Lyons. At the same time, it situates Twain within the influential circle of his family and friends. Skandera-Trombley stakes her claim to Mark Twain (who, she points out, has generally been the property of men), in an effort to redraw the biographical boundaries set by Van Wyck Brooks and Bernard DeVoto. This book includes an exceptional bibliography of primary and secondary works cited.

179. Smith, J. Harold. *Mark Twain: Rebel Pilgrim.* New York: Heath Cote Publishing Corporation, 1973.

This book represents a systematic attempt to chart and integrate Twain's thinking as it evolved through his works and life. This guide to Twain's attitudes and perspectives is organized both chronologically and thematically. Smith focuses on religion and its impact upon Twain's life and work, especially its part in keeping him the constant, though rebellious, pilgrim, always traveling and skeptically searching for the truth. Smith relies heavily upon the work of Albert Bigelow Paine for his facts.

180. Smith, Henry Nash. *Mark Twain: The Development of a Writer.* Cambridge: Harvard University Press, Belknap Press, 1962.

Smith emphasizes Twain's style but also attempts to "demonstrate the interaction between his ideas and attitudes, and the culture that shaped them." He notes that Twain's style reflects his wavering between an acceptance and rejection of conventional attitudes. He covers the whole range of Twain's work, tracing his divided allegiance and ambivalent stances to his style. Smith ultimately draws a picture of a declining artist, one whose inner conflicts lead to a "pathetic" ending.

181. Spengemann, William C. *Mark Twain and the Backwoods Angel: The Matter of Innocence in the Works of Samuel L. Clemens.* Kent: Kent State University Press, 1966.

Although this book primarily describes and investigates the theme of innocence in Mark Twain's writings, it is also a study of Twain's moral and psychological struggle with notions of innocence. Tracing this struggle across the whole range of Twain's works, Spengemann portrays a "mind clinging desperately to traditional values in an age which increasingly denied their validity." Spengemann offers insight into Twain as thinker, providing a means for understanding his often contradictory perspectives, his "romantic hopefulness" and "disenchanted pessimism." The book includes a substantial chapter on Twain's *Personal Recollections of Joan of Arc,* which rarely receives such fair treatment.

182. Stone, Albert E. *The Innocent Eye: Childhood in Mark Twain's Imagination.* New Haven: Yale University Press, 1961.

This study makes some significant claims about Mark Twain as a creative artist and represents a biographical study of his imagination. Stone explores the nature of Twain's mind and the commanding place of childhood experience within it. Stone claims that "childhood" represents the central experience of Twain's life, as it did for many at the turn of the century, and that the author was preoccupied with its depiction. Aside from tracing the theme of childhood in Twain's *The Adventures of Tom Sawyer* and *Adventures of Huckleberry Finn,* Stone examines the often ignored *Personal Recollections of Joan of Arc* and its portrayal of the heroic child. This study allows for a provocative look into Twain's inner life and his participation in the social and intellectual currents of his time.

183. Stonely, Peter. *Mark Twain and the Feminine Aesthetic.* Cambridge: Cambridge University Press, 1992.

This study explores the role that women played in Twain's work and the effect that the notion of the feminine had upon his thought and career. Stonely provides a review of Twain's early career in the opening chapters before turning to a discussion of the author's relationship with specific women. Stonely describes Twain's relations with women in complex and often ironic terms—for example, Twain fostered in his wife the "feminine aesthetic that he so despised in many of his own writings." Other women who Stonely considers in relation to Twain are his daughters, Jean, Susy, and Clara Clemens; Mary Baker Eddy, the founder of Christian Science; his secretary during his final years, Isabel V. Lyon; and the historical and fictional Joan of Arc.

184. Tuckey, John. *Mark Twain and Little Satan: The Writing of* The Mysterious Stranger. West Lafayette: Purdue University Studies, 1963.

This short book provides an intensive study of the *Mysterious Stranger* manuscripts and a "detailed demonstration of the times and circumstances" surrounding their composition. Twain worked on the manuscripts over a period of eleven years, between 1897 and 1908, while enduring some of the greater hardships of his life, most notably the deaths of his daughter and wife. Tuckey reconsiders Twain's later years as he reconstructs the author's preoccupation with his tale of a mysterious stranger, countering a prevailing view of this period of Twain's life as desperate and unproductive.

185. Valentine-Fonorow, Billie. *Was It Heaven or Hell? The Triumphs and Torments of Mark Twain.* Tucson: Fonorow and Associates, 1995.

The question that directs this book is one about Mark Twain's satire. Specifically, the book aims to "relate the circumstances" in Twain's life that occasioned his writing of "Was It Heaven or Was It Hell?" But Valentine-Fonorow also tells Twain's story along the way, devoting chapters to his occupations, family life, career, associations with women, cluster of tragedies, and the author's evolving spirituality. The chapter on "Mark Twain and Women" is especially useful. More on similar topics can be found in book-length studies of each subject, but this book provides a quick reference to pertinent facts and serves as a useful entry point for further exploration.

186. Wiggins, Robert A. *Mark Twain: Jackleg Novelist.* Seattle: University of Washington Press, 1964.

Starting with Twain's reference to himself as a "jackleg" novelist, meaning in this sense a bumbling or incompetent writer, this study portrays both Twain and his work as a peculiar combination of "half assimilated forces" and disassociated thoughts. Twain's is a "primitive mind," Wiggins claims, a product of his Missouri background that lacks the polish of a formal education. Wiggins, however, refrains from drawing Twain as an incompetent impostor but suggests that his life, even his genius, reflects the tensions in his work, the friction between his folk origins and the demands of high literary art.

187. Zall, Paul M. *Mark Twain Laughing: Humorous Anecdotes by and about Samuel L. Clemens.* Knoxville: University of Tennessee Press, 1985.

This book includes a selection of Twain's own recollections and a collection of reminiscences about him. Zall provides all source locations for entries, which are chronologically ordered beginning with an 1851 piece by Twain and continuing to the author's death in 1910 and on through the middle of the twentieth century.

# 5

# Autobiographical Material

*No definitive edition of Mark Twain's autobiography exists, nor is it likely that one ever will. Twain, who had been writing autobiographical pieces for the previous forty years of his life, published a selection of these in the* North American Review *in 1906 and 1907. Others would publish their own versions of Twain's autobiography using Twain's published chapters more or less and a varying assortment of additional autobiographical matter. Twain chose to haphazardly present the story of his life, juxtaposing people and events as he recalled them rather than in some type of chronological order; some scholars followed suit in their own editions of his autobiography, while others have attempted to order Twain's reminiscences in one way or another. Along with Twain's autobiographical writings proper, the following list includes a selection of his fiction that to some degree serves as autobiography.*

## AUTOBIOGRAPHY

188. Kiskis, Michael J. *Mark Twain's Own Autobiography: The Chapters of the* North American Review. Madison: University of Wisconsin Press, 1990.

Twain began writing autobiographical accounts as early as 1870, with his piece on "The Tennessee Land," and he continued to experiment with autobiography until writing "The Death of Jean" in 1909. Much of this material appeared in twenty-five installments for the *North American Review* during 1906 and 1907. Kiskis provides a valuable introduction that discusses Twain's intentions for an autobiography and the author's writing habits as he crafted his stories. Twain chose and revised the installments and approved the pieces for publication, all of which provide a "unified tale" of his life, approved for the public. Kiskis supplies the 1909 essay on Jean, which Twain thought completed his autobiography, in the first appendix. In the second, he supplies a chronological list of autobiographical experiments.

189. Neider, Charles, editor. *The Autobiography of Mark Twain. Including Chapters Now Published for the First Time.* New York: Harper and Row, 1959.

Working from all the manuscript material, Neider brings some sequential order to Twain's stream-of-thought presentation, though in the process of sifting and separating Twain's accounts he admittedly edits out much of what he considered to be "dated, dull," or "trivial." On the other hand, Neider judiciously includes new material from the published and unpublished manuscripts. He provides a note at the beginning of his edition listing the contents of previous editions of Twain's autobiography, allowing for a comparison of selections.

190. Paine, Albert Bigelow. *Mark Twain's Autobiography.* 2 vols. New York: Harper Publishing Company, 1924.

Paine suggests that Twain began to formally piece together his autobiographical writings while in Vienna, from 1897 to 1899. This book attempts to deliver such memoirs and other later recollections in much the same manner that Twain presented them. Thus, Paine's two-volume edition presents Twain's writings and dictations as a selection of memories loosely connected as associative ideas. Twain believed he was producing a new kind of autobiography, one that would freely express the events of his life as his current thinking reshaped them. As his mind roamed back and forth across personal and historical landscape, Twain recorded and elaborated upon some of the more significant biographical markers. Later editors would attempt to impose some order upon Twain's experimental style, but Paine's edition faithfully adheres to his spontaneous delivery.

## RELATED AUTOBIOGRAPHICAL SOURCES

191. Chowder, Ken, editor. *Goldmines and Guttersnipes: Tales of California by Mark Twain.* San Francisco: Chronicle Books, 1991.

In his introduction to this selection of letters and newspaper articles, Chowder offers a biographical summary of Twain's western experience. The letters, written mostly for California newspapers while Twain was in San Francisco between 1863 and 1866, relate some of the high points of Twain's life as a journalist. His descriptions of California earthquakes are especially vivid and his correspondence covering his travels and friends useful and detailed. Some of the topics Chowder covers are "Politics," "Forty-Niners," "Religion and Morality," "In the House of the Spirits," and "Travels in California." This book includes excerpts from *Roughing It* and Twain's lectures.

192. Clemens, Cyril. *Mark Twain: The Letter Writer.* Boston: Meador Publishing Company, 1932.

The purpose of this book, as its author tells us, is to offer a few "intimate glimpses" of Mark Twain and a few curious accounts and recollections of the author as well. This it does, arranging select letters and accounts in chronological order beginning with an 1868 letter that finds Twain begging a friend to help him protect his lectures from journalistic summaries. The book concludes with a 1910 letter written by Twain while in Bermuda, a note of thanks to a "Cousin Katherine" for her concern and prayers for him. In between, the letters are separated into chapters that focus on particular years, places, or themes. Clemens's commentary locates the letters within their biographical context and, to some extent, explains their reason for being. Some of Twain's recollections reveal what Clemens calls the "soul of [the] man," such as E. P. Proudfit's story of Twain's obsession with the Orchestrelle and his general craving for moving musical pieces. This book includes a wide-ranging index.

193. DeVoto, Bernard. *Mark Twain in Eruption. Hitherto Unpublished Pages about Men and Events.* New York: Harper and Brothers Publishers, 1940.

In this edition of Twain's writings, DeVoto collects the memoirs that Albert Bigelow Paine edited out of his 1924 publication of Twain's autobiography. Choosing to ignore Twain's free-association method of recording his memories, DeVoto rearranges the mainly unpublished portions of the author's autobiography under relevant headings. To DeVoto's credit, his presentation does help establish thematic relationships and Twain's involvement with significant people and places. Such relationships fall beneath the following chapter headings: "Theodore Roosevelt," "Andrew Carnegie," "The Plutocracy," "Hannibal Days," "Two Halos," "In a Writer's Workshop," "Various Literary People," "The Last Visit to England," and "Miscellany." DeVoto describes his book more as a presentation of "a kind of table talk" rather than an autobiography, a record of Twain discussing people and events and his relation to them.

194. Evans, John D. *A Tom Sawyer Companion: An Autobiographical Guided Tour with Mark Twain.* Lanham, Md.: University Press of America, 1993.

Twain's boyhood years weave their way throughout the pages of *The Adventures of Tom Sawyer.* The places, events, and characters that find a fictional life in the book point back to the reality of Twain's boyhood. Evans systematically reads *Tom Sawyer,* summarizing important scenes, making direct connections between scenes and Twain's boyhood, and finally relating both text and facts to Twain's own recollections of his Hannibal youth. The book as a whole traces what Twain himself fictionally recorded as some of the most significant events of his life; at the same time, it documents the reality of the fictional matter by comparing Twain's account and those of his family and friends with his novel's record of experiences. Evans's inclusion of relevant photographs provides an even more exact documentation of Twain's childhood experiences.

195. Fatout, Paul, editor. *Mark Twain: Speaks for Himself.* West Lafayette: Purdue University Press, 1978.

Although not intentionally a narrative of Twain's development as a writer and thinker, this collection of his writings, as Fatout suggests, might be read as such a story. Arranged chronologically, these various newspaper and magazine pieces span most of Twain's writing career, beginning with his work for the *Territorial Enterprise* and extending to his last years.

196. McKeithan, Daniel Morley, editor. *Traveling with the Innocents Abroad: Mark Twain's Original Reports from Europe and the Holy Land.* Norman: University of Oklahoma Press, 1958.

For more than five months in 1867, Twain traveled throughout Europe, the Holy Land, and Egypt; as a special correspondent for the *Daily Alta California,* he recorded his observations for its readers. All of Twain's letters to the *Daily Alta,* along with a few written for other newspapers, are included in this volume. Twain did include his reports in *The Innocents Abroad*—in revised or polished form; McKeithan presents them as originally written. He also provides explanatory notes that indicate deletions, additions, and specific textual alterations, since Twain "did not reprint a single letter verbatim."

## AUTOBIOGRAPHICAL FICTION

197. Twain, Mark. *The Adventures of Tom Sawyer.* Hartford: American Publishing Company, 1876.

In this novel Twain relies heavily upon his boyhood experiences and the people and events of his young life in Hannibal, Missouri. Although he embellishes his memories for the necessities of fiction, he did live through some of his hero's ordeals, such as childhood romances and the unholy demands of formal education. Laura Hawkins, Twain's childhood sweetheart, was in fact Twain's model for Tom's dream girl, Becky Thatcher.

198. Twain, Mark. *Following the Equator: A Journey around the World.* Hartford: American Publishing Company, 1897.

On July 14, 1895, Twain began the first part of a lecture tour through North America that would eventually take him as far away as Australia, New Zealand, India, and South Africa. His world lecture tour ended on July 15, 1896. The tour was primarily undertaken by Twain as a means for settling bankruptcy claims against him, which were paid with the tour's and book's earnings. Twain rarely embellishes his experiences in this book as he tells about the people and places he encountered, resorting more to his early journalistic style of writing. However, the facts do provide Twain room for ongoing commentary on customs and events.

199. Twain, Mark, and Charles Dudley Warner. *The Gilded Age: A Tale of Today.* Hartford: American Publishing Company, 1874.

According to legend, Twain and Warner began writing this book on a challenge from their wives to write something better than the usual novels then popular. Having taken the challenge, Twain and Warner wrote and collated their individual contributions to the book, with Twain drawing on his family history for some parts of his chapters. He freely adapted character traits from his relatives, especially from his father and brother Orion, and generally retold his family's move from back East to the Missouri countryside.

200. Twain, Mark. *Innocents Abroad, or The New Pilgrim's Progress; Being Some Account of the Steamship* Quaker City*'s Pleasure Excursion to Europe and the Holy Land.* Hartford: American Publishing Company, 1869.

For the most part, Twain crafted this book around letters that he wrote for the *San Francisco Alta California* while he was touring abroad at the newspaper's expense. Although the letters recorded his daily adventures throughout Europe and the Holy Land, Twain selectively shaped and presented the characters and events he felt worth remembering for his book. When necessary, he added and deleted information.

201. Twain, Mark. *Life on the Mississippi.* Boston: James R. Osgood, 1883.

From February 1857 to May 1861, Mark Twain served as either an apprentice cub or a fully licensed steamboat pilot on the Mississippi River. In the first part of this book, taken from "Old Times on the Mississippi," Twain recalls and elaborates on his early days as a cub pilot; his trials and successes; and especially his relationship with Horace Bixby, a man determined to either teach him the river or kill him. In the rest of the book, Twain recalls and comments on the experience of returning to the river in 1882.

202. Twain, Mark. *Roughing It.* Hartford: American Publishing Company, 1872.

For more than five years in the 1860s, Twain roamed throughout the West, primarily in Nevada and California. This book presents the high points of that experience though, as usual, Twain shapes and refigures many of the events and characters involved in his travels. Nonetheless, the book generally establishes an accurate account of important facts relating to Twain's adventures, beginning with his stagecoach trip westward with his brother Orion, his meetings with famous and infamous people, mining fiascoes, newspaper positions, and his travels even farther westward to the Sandwich Islands.

203. Twain, Mark. *A Tramp Abroad.* Hartford: American Publishing Company, 1880.

For nearly seventeen months, between April 1878 and August 1879, Twain traveled about Europe with his family. He recorded a vast amount of notes about his experiences while on this journey, intending to include them in *A Tramp Abroad.* Many were, and Twain occasionally lets his narrative drift in and out of specific recollections about his career and former travels. His narrative is especially useful for tracing his path through Germany and Switzerland. His time in the latter, where he climbed around the Alps with his good friend Joseph Twichell, fills more than fifteen chapters in this book.

6

# Letters, Notebooks, and Speeches

*You can learn quite a bit about Twain's life from his letters or by reading his personal and public observations. The books in this chapter present such material, revealing not only the events and people that influenced Twain but also the thoughts and emotions of Twain himself. Much of this material has been collected by the* Mark Twain Papers *project of the University of California at Berkeley.*

204. Anderson, Frederick, Michael B. Frank, and Kenneth M. Sanderson. *Mark Twain's Notebooks and Journals: Volume 1, 1855–1873.* Berkeley and Los Angeles: University of California Press, 1975.

    Mark Twain's journals contain a wealth of detail about Twain's life and help indicate how he refashioned his experiences into the narratives for which he is best known. Albert Bigelow Paine published an incomplete volume of Twain's notebooks in 1935, but this book is the first in a multivolume project that will provide all forty-nine of Twain's notebooks. This volume, covering twelve notebooks in all, ranges over an eighteen-year period and begins with a few notes about French lessons that the young Sam Clemens recorded in 1855; it continues with the notes he recorded while a steamboat cub pilot and while in the West, in the Sandwich Islands (Hawaii), in Europe, and back in San Francisco and then New York. The headnote for each notebook chapter provides a general discussion of the contents of the notes, while extensive footnotes explain and document notebook material. Notebook entries, for the most part, are presented in their original form.

205. Anderson, Frederick, Lin Salamo, and Bernard L. Stein. *Mark Twain's Notebooks and Journals: Volume 2, 1877–1883.* Berkeley and Los Angeles: University of California Press, 1975.

    Notebooks, if they exist, have yet to be found for the four years preceding the ones in this volume. These nine notebooks refer mostly to Twain's travels to Bermuda, Europe, and back to the Mississippi River. Like the first volume in this set, this volume includes extensive footnotes and useful explanations of Twain's stylistic habits.

206. Branch, Edgar M., editor. *Mark Twain's Letters in the* Muscatine Journal. Chicago: Mark Twain Association of America, 1942.
This collection contains five letters of Mark Twain's that were written between 1853 and 1855 to the M*uscatine Journal.* In his introduction, Branch discusses Twain's experience as a journalist before his trip west to Nevada and San Francisco.

207. Branch, Edgar M., Michael B. Frank, and Kenneth M. Sanderson, editors. *Mark Twain's Letters: Volume 1, 1853–1866.* Berkeley and Los Angeles: University of California Press, 1988.
This first volume of Twain's letters is one in a series of projected volumes to be published by the Mark Twain Project of the University of California's Bancroft Library. These volumes are part of the *Mark Twain Papers* and represent the exhaustive efforts of dedicated Twain scholars. Aside from the letters, each volume includes a wealth of scholarly commentary and appendix matter supplementing the letters with photographs, manuscript facsimiles, maps, relevant calendars, and other informative material. Explanatory notes accompany each letter, and the indexing and referencing for all volumes is thorough and meticulous. The first letter in this volume was written in 1853 by the seventeen-year-old Sam Clemens attempting to explain his rambling habits and some of the curiosities of New York to his mother. The volume closes in 1866 with another letter to his mother; the seasoned journalist is roving again, this time as a correspondent for the *San Francisco Alta California.* The letters that span these thirteen years spring from Twain's experiences as a printer, steamboat pilot and steersman, gold and silver miner, and western journalist, to name only his primary occupations. The letters also document Twain's development as a writer and thinker.

208. Cooley, John, ed. *Mark Twain's Aquarium: The Samuel Clemens Angelfish Correspondence, 1905–1910.* Athens: University of Georgia Press, 1991.
The "Aquarium" was an informal club for girls who had been especially chosen by Mark Twain as "Angelfish," a nickname he

gave to a group of girls that he had met, mostly by chance, who seemed somehow representative of the purity and innocence of childhood. Over the last five years of his life, Twain kept in close contact with this select group, eventually numbering a dozen or so, visiting, corresponding, and even vacationing with them and their parents. Along with the three hundred known letters that make up the correspondence between Twain and his Angelfish, which are chronologically arranged, Cooley provides introductory remarks for different chapter groupings of the letters, placing them within the context of Twain's association with particular girls. The book includes photographs of several members of Twain's Aquarium and a listing and present location of relevant letters.

209. Day, A. Grove. *Mark Twain's Letters from Hawaii.* Honolulu: University of Hawaii Press, 1975.

This volume recounts Twain's visit to the Sandwich Islands, in July 1866, while he was a newspaper correspondent for the *Sacramento Union.* The letters add to Twain's recollections as found in *Roughing It* and are particularly useful for understanding his developing views on Christianity, democracy, and political power. Twain would return to the islands in 1895.

210. Fatout, Paul, editor. *Mark Twain Speaking.* Iowa City: University of Iowa Press, 1976.

Fatout includes an informative discussion of Twain's lecturing habits in his introduction to this hefty volume of Twain's speeches. As Fatout points out, Twain's speeches reveal the extent to which he could teach and preach to his audience, mock and denounce shams, and uplift the sincere. Fatout provides headnotes to each selection, setting the speech in the context of time, place, and event. Footnotes also clarify any important names and places mentioned in the speeches as well as their publication dates and places. The book includes a chronology of Twain's speeches, plus explanatory notes dating from 1856 through 1909 and an unusually thorough index of people and places.

211. Fischer, Victor, and Michael B. Frank, editors. *Mark Twain's Letters: Volume 3, 1869.* Berkeley and Los Angeles: University of California Press, 1992.

This edition includes 188 of Twain's letters, most published for the first time. As might be expected at this stage of Twain's life, a large percentage of the letters are written to Olivia Langdon. His letters to his future wife were increasing in length as his love and desire intensified. In a letter dated January 22, 1869, he sent Livy kisses "on the night wind" to find and imaginatively provoke her; in a later letter, May 9, he writes that he is not "capable of loving any other woman" but her; and on September 7, he writes of soon enjoying her as his "own Livy for time and eternity." His letters to Olivia and others also reveal the pains and pleasures of the lecture circuit, as Twain found himself lecturing throughout the East and Midwest. Appendixes include material about the lectures that had been enclosed in the letters, a "Calendar of Courtship Letters: 1868–1870," a "Lecture Schedule, 1868–1870," "Advertising Circulars," and "Photographs and Manuscript Facsimiles." Like the other volumes in this ongoing publication of Twain's letters, this edition provides through and meticulous textual commentaries and documentation.

212. Fischer, Victor, and Michael B. Frank, editors. *Mark Twain's Letters: Volume 4, 1870–1871.* Berkeley and Los Angeles: University of California Press, 1995.

This volume begins with a letter from Twain to Olivia Langdon, written January 6, 1870. Twain is finishing a lecture tour and is anxious to return to his fiancée, whom he will marry on February 2, 1870. The concluding letter in this volume finds Twain on yet another tour, writing home to Hartford and Olivia once more. Most of the letters in this volume are published for the first time and extend through his life in Buffalo, New York, where he was a part owner and coeditor of the *Buffalo Express,* on to a brief residence in Elmira, New York, and finally to Hartford, Connecticut. A major portion of the letters in this volume are written by Twain to his wife, to his brother, Orion, and to Elisha Bliss, who was preparing to publish *Roughing It.*

213. Hill, Hamlin, editor. *Mark Twain's Letters to His Publishers, 1867–1894.* Berkeley and Los Angeles: University of California Press, 1967.

In all, 290 letters are offered in this volume, representing primarily the correspondence between Twain and his three chief publishers: Elisha Bliss, James R. Osgood, and Charles L. Webster. These letters record Twain's complex involvement with the publication of his work and his often antagonistic relations with his publishers. Hill divides the letters into appropriate chapters and provides biographical details for understanding them within the context of Twain's business interests.

214. Leary, Lewis, editor. *Mark Twain's Correspondence with Henry Huttleston Rogers, 1893–1909.* Berkeley: University of California Press, 1969.

This book provides all the known correspondence between Twain and the man who would become his close friend and financial advisor during his later, often tumultuous, years. H. H. Rogers, one of America's wealthiest industrialists, befriended Twain at a time when the author was near financial ruin and gradually helped him to reclaim his respect and financial security. Although this Standard Oil Company executive was considered by some to be a ruthless businessman, Twain knew Rogers as the "best friend" he ever had and the "only man [he] would give a damn for." This collection of 462 letters documents the business and personal relations shared by the two men. As with other volumes supported by the Mark Twain Project, this edition represents a meticulously edited and scholarly addition to the ongoing publication of Twain material. The introduction to the book provides a brief but factual explanation of the relationship between Twain and Rogers, and Leary introduces each chapter with further information necessary for understanding the correspondence. The appendixes include the financial agreements drawn up by Rogers that in large part saved Twain from financial ruin.

215. Leary, Lewis, editor. *Mark Twain's Letters to Mary.* New York: Columbia University Press, 1961.

In this collection of letters from Twain to Mary Benjamin Rogers, Leary uses contemporary accounts of Twain's activities and biographical material from Albert Bigelow Paine, Clara Clemens, and Bernard DeVoto to tell the story of one of Twain's later and more endearing friendships. The letters were written between 1900 and 1910, with all but one during the last four years of the author's life, and illustrate how much Twain needed Rogers's inspiration during a painful period. The letters also expose an intimate and affectionate side of Twain.

216. Paine, Albert Bigelow, editor. *Mark Twain's Letters.* 2 vols. New York: Harper and Brothers Publishers, 1917.

Paine calls his collection of Twain's letters "reasonably complete," and while his edition of the letters does cover nearly sixty years of the author's life—from 1853 until 1910—much was edited within the letters or selectively ignored by Paine. Nonetheless, as the recent editors of the more scholarly project to publish Twain's letters acknowledge, Paine's edition remains an "indispensable" source, and Paine himself the "sole source" for our knowledge of Twain's correspondence. Paine's comments throughout the text explain and, at times, interpret events within particular biographical contexts. Paine includes a selective index of names and subjects.

217. Paine, Albert Bigelow, editor. *Mark Twain's Notebook.* New York: Harper and Brothers, 1935.

Paine had included some of the material found here in his biography of Mark Twain, but he offers a fuller range of the author's thought in this edition of his journal notes. Paine's foreword points out that this provides no surprises. It is his intent, rather, to offer Mark Twain "at his best and at his worst." Paine selects and presents the entries, which cover nearly the last fifty years of the author's life, in chronological order and primarily in relation to Twain's travels: beginning with Twain's time on the Mississippi River and later as a western miner, moving through his adventures in Hawaii and his travels abroad, then his literary life back home, on to his European travels in the 1890s and his return to America, and up until a couple of years before his death. Paine provides biographical commentary throughout, locating Twain's notes in context to their time and place. The book includes an index of names and places.

218. Salamo, Lin, and Harriet Elinor Smith, editors. *Mark Twain's Letters: Volume 5, 1872–1873.* Berkeley and Los Angeles: University of California Press, 1997.

The more than three hundred letters in this volume begin with Twain's letter to James Redpath on January 2, 1872, and conclude with his letter to Redpath on December 31, 1873. Redpath was Twain's lecture promoter and had organized successful tours for the author in the winters of 1869–1870 and 1871–1872. He was just one of the many friends Twain corresponded with during 1872 and 1873, however. Others were the successful Bret Harte; William Dean Howells, who was then the editor of the *Atlantic Monthly;* and Charles Dudley Warner, with whom he would write and publish *The Gilded Age.* Twain's travels continued, and his letters reveal the many friends he made around the world.

219. Smith, Harriet Elinor, and Richard Bucci, editors. *Mark Twain's Letters: Volume 2, 1867–1868.* Berkeley and Los Angeles: University of California Press, 1990.

A little more than 150 letters are collected in this volume and, as its editors point out, these provide a "detailed and candid account" of Twain's transformation from a western journalist and lecturer to a fledgling author poised to receive national recognition and the blessings of eastern culture. Twain's first book, *The Celebrated Jumping Frog of Calaveras County and Other Sketches,* was published during the time covered by this collection, and he completed the tour of Europe and the Holy Land that would provide material for *The Innocents Abroad.* Many of the final letters in this volume center on his introduction to and early courtship of Olivia Langdon. Some notable material in the appendixes includes a list of "Passengers and Crew of the *Quaker City,*" an "Itinerary of the *Quaker City* Excursion," "Enclosures with the Letters," the "Contract for *The Innocents Abroad,*" Twain's "Lecture Schedule, 1868–1869," and "Photographs and Manuscript Facsimiles."

220. Smith, Henry Nash, and William Gibson. *Mark Twain–Howells Letters: The Correspondence of Samuel L. Clemens and William D. Howells, 1872–1910.* 2 vols. Cambridge: Harvard University Press, Belknap Press, 1960.

This two-volume set contains the complete collection of letters known to have passed between Twain and Howells between 1872 and 1910. Their friendship remains one of the most remarkable in the history of American life and letters, and their correspondence reveals how much each man learned from the other. Much can be gathered from these letters about the extent to which Howells's critical advice furthered Twain's career. At the same time, the letters reveal the lively spark Twain brought into Howells's life in general. There are informative footnotes and a substantial appendix section with a calendar of letters and discussions of work Howells critiqued for Twain. The "biographical directory," with its brief sketches of those people most mentioned in the letters, is especially useful.

221. Wecter, Dixon. *The Love Letters of Mark Twain.* New York: Harper and Brothers, 1949.

This collection reveals Twain's evolving relationship with Olivia Langdon and the Langdon family. The letters portray Twain as sensitive and eloquent, and his future wife as understanding and perceptive. Wecter believes the letters will "refute certain misconceptions" about the relationship between Twain and Olivia Langdon, the most damaging being that she was a domineering critic and censor of her husband's work. This book includes an identifying list of people mentioned in the letters and a checklist of all known letters from Twain to Olivia Langdon.

222. Wecter, Dixon, editor. *Mark Twain to Mrs. Fairbanks.* San Marino, Calif.: Huntington Library Publications, 1949.

Wecter prefaces this collection of Twain's letters by pointing out the influential role Mary Mason Fairbanks had in Twain's shift from western journalist to professional author. As these letters reveal, Twain found comfort in confiding in "Mother Fairbanks," whom he first met on the *Quaker City* cruise and who accepted the role Twain opened for her as his moral guide. Wecter organizes his collection by three primary topics, "The Courtship of Livy," "The New Household," and "The Busy Years." Twain continued his correspondence with Fairbanks from 1867 until a few years before her death in 1898. This book includes especially detailed annotations and pertinent commentary throughout.

7

# Related Biographical Sources

*Mark Twain is discussed in numerous books to one degree or another. The entries below refer to sketches, pamphlets, and books that provide varying amounts of information on Twain. Some are studies of humor or American traits, while others offer evaluations of authors or literary genres, and still others are biographies of some who knew Twain. Each book offers a different perspective on Twain's life and perhaps a little-known fact or two.*

223. Ade, George. *One Afternoon with Mark Twain.* Chicago: Mark Twain Society of Chicago, 1939

Although George Ade and Mark Twain met only once, in 1902, Ade would remember his brief visit with the "all time Dean of American Literature" as the "most momentous meeting of [his] life." His "few impressions," recorded here in fifteen pages, recall a cordial and relaxed Twain at home in New York and, at the same time, a more serious and thoughtful man than he had expected. This booklet is written more as a tribute than as an informative biographical sketch.

224. Blair, Walter. *Native American Humor, 1800–1900.* New York: American Book Company, 1937.

The first part of this book, nearly two hundred pages, traces the development of an American tradition of humor through its nineteenth-century growing pains and on toward its peak moments at the century's turn. Blair meticulously follows the various strains of American humor, its eastern and western revisions, its rhetorical convolutions through the mouths of literary comedians, through the dialectic fashioning of local colorists, and on to its most successful purveyor: Mark Twain. Blair discusses Twain's debt to the humor of the Old Southwest on pages 147–62, and after linking Twain firmly within the Southwestern tradition, he notes the author's ability to transcend traditional literary boundaries and turn his comic sense toward the demands of the encroaching twentieth century.

225. Blair, Walter, and Hamlin Hill. *America's Humor: From Poor Richard to Doonesbury.* New York: Oxford University Press, 1978.

This book maps the terrain of American humor from its earliest beginnings in colonial times to its latest expression in the twentieth century. It particularly investigates the way humor participates in the shaping of American history and interacts with significant social, political, and intellectual events. Blair and Hill devote two chapters to Mark Twain, pages 303–63, locating his comic techniques in their literary and historical context. His more famous shorter pieces and some of his lesser-read longer books, including *The American Claimant, The Gilded Age,* and *Personal Recollections of Joan of Arc,* are discussed along with his more popular and critically acclaimed *Huckleberry Finn, A Connecticut Yankee,* and *Pudd'nhead Wilson.* Blair and Hill conclude with an account of Twain as a forerunner of twentieth-century humor, as they point to his later experiments with comic devices for countering a peculiarly modern sense of despair. Includes an extensive list of references with brief notes on the value of the sources.

226. Bradford, Gamaliel. *American Portraits, 1875–1900.* Boston: Houghton Mifflin Company, 1922.

A chapter on Mark Twain begins this collection, which also includes such other notable Americans as Henry Adams, Henry James, and Grover Cleveland. Gamaliel Bradford's intention is to present "representative figures in all varied lines of life." To this end, on pages 3–28 he strings together an account of Twain that draws him as a homegrown genius of sorts—not necessarily a great thinker, but an energetic artist who profited from sporadic flashes of great insight. Nonetheless, Bradford ranks Twain with Cervantes and Shakespeare as a comic genius. Bradford offers no dates for Twain's writings or events mentioned as central to his life. His is more of an intimate attempt to understand the mind, soul, and character of the man he affectionately calls "Mark."

227. Brooks, Cleanth, R. W. B. Lewis, and Robert Penn Warren. *American Literature: The Makers and Making.* New York: St. Martin's Press, 1974.

This is a multivolume textbook/anthology aimed at undergraduates or the general reader. It emphasizes the writer, the literature, and the reader's response to both. The section on Twain, pages 1261–92, is a highly reliable sketch of the author's life and a discussion of his major novels within the context of that life. What emerges is a harmonious overview of Twain's growth as a writer. The Twain section includes a biographical chart and bibliography that focuses on biographies.

228. Covici, Pascal, Jr. *Humor and Revelation in American Literature: The Puritan Connection.* Columbia: University of Missouri Press, 1997.

While this book is aimed primarily at unearthing the roots of American humor and establishing to what degree these spring from Puritan sources, it does contain some information on Twain's connection to certain traditions and lines of thought. In fact, Covici uses Twain's experience at the *Atlantic* dinner in December 1877 and the "Whittier Birthday Speech" he delivered there as a type of paradigm for his discussion of the effects of Puritan thought on American humor in general. Covici's book, then, serves as a vantage point from which readers can more thoroughly appreciate the landscape of Twain's comic sense.

229. Elliott, Emory, general editor. *Columbia Literary History of the United States.* New York: Columbia University Press, 1988.

On pages 627–44 of this volume, Philip Fisher provides his entry on Twain. Fisher concentrates on Twain's life after the Civil War and his part in the late-nineteenth-century "material world of wealth." Fisher's portrait draws Twain as a public figure and popular entertainer whose self-promotion, to a large degree, helped him to succeed.

230. Frederick, John T. *The Darkened Sky: Nineteenth-Century American Novelists and Religion.* Notre Dame: University of Notre Dame Press, 1969.

In this book, Frederick examines the ways in which major American novelists responded to the various and often conflicting religious perspectives that flourished in nineteenth-century America. His choice of those writers who were particularly responsive to religious problems include James Fenimore Cooper, Nathaniel Hawthorne, Herman Melville, William Dean Howells, Henry James, and Mark Twain. After establishing some of the major reasons for the religious tensions recurrent in the novels of these writers—such as biblical scholarship, theories of evolution, and a proliferation of religious sects, to name the crucial ones—Frederick draws revealing parallels between the expression of religious attitudes in the novels and the lives of their authors. This method is quite revealing in Frederick's section on Twain, which appears on pages 123–76.

231. Gardner, Joseph. *Dickens in America: Twain, Howells, James, and Norris.* New York: Garland Publishing, 1988.

A substantial amount of this book—pages 17–115—is devoted to exploring Mark Twain's response to Charles Dickens. Gardner offers an incisive discussion of events surrounding Twain's criticism of Dickens, in particular, combing Twain's letters and notebooks for relevant remarks and observations. Twain had some personal contact with Dickens family members but not directly with the renowned English author, although Gardner links the two men at particular times and events. Gardner's book is not a study of direct influence, however. Rather, in demonstrating that Twain and Dickens had similar visions, attitudes, and expressive methods, this book illuminates the thought of both authors.

232. Gibson, William. *Theodore Roosevelt among the Humorists: W. D. Howells, Mark Twain, and Mr. Dooley.* Knoxville: University of Tennessee Press, 1980.

A major portion of this book focuses on Twain's relations and reactions to Theodore Roosevelt. In particular, Gibson points to Twain's return to America in 1900, after his world lecture tour, as an initial stage in Twain's relations with Roosevelt. These relations might be described as "strained" at best. Twain found himself more and more in conflict with Roosevelt's foreign policy, and Gibson clearly details the incidents surrounding Twain's part in the national and political debates of his day. Includes some material on Twain's anti-imperialist activities.

233. Gillis, James M. *False Prophets.* Chicago: Extension Press, 1927.

In a book that derides the value of writers and thinkers such as G. B. Shaw, Sigmund Freud, H. G. Wells, and Friedrich Nietzsche, Gillis finds a place for Mark Twain as well. Gillis is out to dethrone those who undermine traditional concepts of God and religion, and in his chapter on Twain, on pages 125–45, he portrays the author as an "inveterate pessimist" and "hater of the human race." Rather than using raw facts, however, Gillis mostly draws his conclusions about Twain's life through reading only a few of the author's major works. Twain has rarely been drawn in a darker light.

234. Girgus, Sam B., editor. *The American Self: Myth, Ideology, and Popular Culture.* Albuquerque: University of New Mexico, 1981.

Walter Blair, well known for his work on American humor, contributes the essay on Mark Twain for this collection: "Mark Twain and the Mind's Ear." In the essay, on pages 231–39, Blair explores Twain's development as a writer, arguing that Twain's remarks on other writers cast an informative light on his own creative habits and techniques. He goes on to relate Twain the writer to the author's performance as a public figure in an effort to recapture a more authentic experience of writer and humorist.

235. Greenslet, Ferris. *The Life of Thomas Bailey Aldrich.* Boston: Houghton Mifflin Company, 1908.

Between 1881 and 1890, Thomas Bailey Aldrich served as the editor of the *Atlantic Monthly,* although he may be best known for his book about childhood, *The Story of a Bad Boy* (1869). Twain claimed to not have been influenced by the book, though his characterization of Tom Sawyer resembles that of Aldrich's own boy hero. Twain and Aldrich began their lifelong friendship in 1871, and Greenslet includes some of their correspondence, along with a few anecdotes about Twain, in his biographical study of Aldrich. Greenslet also provides a self-portrait drawn by Twain in 1874.

236. Hagedorn, Hermann. *Americans: A Book of Lives.* New York: John Day Company, 1946.

This collection of brief biographies includes among its select luminaries Thomas Edison, Booker T. Washington, John Dewey, Helen Keller, Will Rogers, Franklin D. Roosevelt, and, in its opening chapter, Mark Twain (pages 3–17). These are stories of great lives, according to Hagedorn, that mirror the "American mind and American heart." Twain's chapter portrays him as important to his time as a humorist who brought needed relief and a "cleansing laughter" to a country emerging from civil strife. Like the other portraits in this collection, Twain's concludes on an optimistic tone, showing him to embody the stamina and resiliency that this book as a whole identifies as American.

237. Kazin, Alfred. *An American Procession.* New York: Alfred A. Knopf, 1984.

This book provides an interpretation of some of the major figures in American literature, beginning in the 1830s with Emerson and continuing through the first half of the twentieth century and the American literary modernists. In his chapter on Mark Twain, on pages 181–210, Kazin underscores the author's literary talent and background as a writer, his influences, and his successes and later life anxieties. He portrays Twain as an adept writer and performer and offers some evidence for Twain as a manipulator of circumstances.

238. King, Grace. *Memories of a Southern Woman of Letters.* New York: Macmillan Company, 1932.

King visited Mark Twain and his family at their home in Hartford, Connecticut, and vacationed with them in Florence, Italy, in 1892. Some of her memories in this book look back on her time with Twain and his family. King includes one of Twain's letters.

239. Lee, Brian. *American Fiction, 1865–1940.* New York: Longman, 1987.

Lee discusses Mark Twain first in this volume that offers a general introduction to seventy-five years of American fiction. Twain's chapter, on pages 14–26, opens with a brief biographical record of major events in the author's life; it follows with a study of Twain's major fiction, connecting his characters and fictional worlds to historical events and the author's public and private life. This book includes notes on Twain biographies and criticism.

240. Moss, Joyce, and George Wilson. *Profiles in American History: Significant Events and the People Who Shaped Them.* 8 vols. Detroit: Gale Research, U X L, 1994.

This series is especially aimed at high school students and includes portraits, maps, selections from primary sources, and contextual information related to select personalities. The article on Twain appears in volume 5, "Reconstruction to the Spanish American War," pages 158–71. There are a few pages on Twain's personal background before a discussion of his participation in American literature as a literary realist. The article blends major events in Twain's life, such as his many occupations and his marriage, with the writing of his major works. Also included are photographs and illustrations from some of Twain's books.

241. Parks, Edd Winfield. *Segments of Southern Thought.* Athens: University of Georgia Press, 1938.

This collection of essays is intended to be "suggestive" rather than definitive. In the discussion on Twain (pages 245–49), Parks suggests the need for a different kind of biography of Mark Twain, one that explores his southern sympathies. He points out Twain's reliance on his memories of the South for much of his work and suggests that the author was uneasy in the North, far from the "people who might have understood him." He maintains that Twain could not "integrate himself into a new life," but only recall memories of his former one. This book warrants inclusion here for its comments on what Parks sees as an ambivalent allegiance to northern values and lifestyle.

242. Phelps, William Lyon. *Some Makers of American Literature.* New York: Books for Libraries Press, 1970.

This is a reprint of the original 1923 edition, which is a collection of Phelps's lectures on a few major American authors. The lecture on Mark Twain concludes the collection, which also contains talks on Cooper, Lincoln, Hawthorne, and Emerson. Phelps's recollections of Twain reflect his own boyhood experience in Hartford, Connecticut. He remembers, for instance, seeing Twain as the author went for his strolls down the streets of Hartford, a powerful figure for all his 5' 8" frame, with shaggy hair amassed high on his head and his sealskin coat turned inside out.

243. Pizer, Donald, editor. *Hamlin Garland's Diaries.* San Marino, Calif.: Huntington Library, 1968.

Although not a close friend, Hamlin Garland had heard Twain speak when he was a student and had interviewed the author in

London in 1899. He mentions Twain a few times in his diaries and provides glimpses of him as he lived out his last few years. Garland's notes paint a rather bleak portrait of an old and feeble Mark Twain.

244. Rourke, Constance. *American Humor: A Study of the National Character.* New York: Harcourt Brace Jovanovich, 1931.

In this wide-ranging study of a particular literary history, Rourke traces the roots of American humor from its Yankee beginnings, through its frontier transformations, its literary appropriations, and on to its implicit shaping of American thought and character. Within what Rourke sees as a consistent, though shifting, native tradition, she posits Mark Twain as the recipient of the fullest expression of that tradition. In her discussion of Twain, on pages 209–21, Rourke reviews Twain's experiences on the western frontier and his debt to an American tradition of humor.

245. Smith, Henry Nash. *Democracy and the Novel: Popular Resistance to Classic American Literature Writers.* New York: Oxford University Press, 1978.

Maintaining Santayana's position that an intimate connection exists between "philosophical ideas and literary practice," Smith argues in this book that Twain's style reveals his inmost self. The beliefs and thoughts that helped frame Twain's philosophical being can be traced to his divided sympathies, as Smith contends, especially to his understanding of both "high culture" and "folk culture" values. Smith reveals how this dual allegiance to opposing cultures continued to emerge in Twain's stylistic maneuvers and how stylistic changes, themselves, continued to represent the author's developing philosophies. Smith concludes his study of Twain, found primarily on pages 104–27, by making some intriguing, biographically illuminating connections between Twain and writers as seemingly diverse as Emerson and Thomas Pynchon.

246. Strong, Leah A. *Joseph Hopkins Twichell: Mark Twain's Friend and Pastor.* Athens: University of Georgia Press, 1966.

In 1867, Joseph Twichell and Mark Twain began their friendship, which would continue to grow until Twain's death in 1910. At different times in their relationship, Twichell acted as Twain's reader, advisor, and traveling companion. While this book tells the story of Twichell's life, it includes a significant amount of discussion about Twain and Twichell's influence on the author.

247. Taylor, Coley B. *Mark Twain's Margins on Thackeray's* Swift. New York: Gotham House, 1935.

Mark Twain's last official place of residence was at his "Stormfield" mansion in Redding, Connecticut. Taylor was only a child while he lived at Redding, but he vividly recalls seeing and hearing about his famous neighbor. He devotes nearly half of this book to his recollections and the rest to Twain's marginal comments on Thackeray's *Swift.* He offers, then, both an intimate view of Twain as a citizen of Redding and a portrait of Twain as a literary critic.

248. Varble, Rachel M. *Jane Clemens: The Story of Mark Twain's Mother.* Garden City, N.Y.: Doubleday and Company, 1964.

References to Samuel Clemens in this book are nearly as numerous as those to its primary subject, Jane Clemens. In fact, some of the details that Varble supplies about the young Sam Clemens are not generally discussed elsewhere. Passages and sections devoted to Twain are drawn, as might be expected, in relation to Jane Clemens and her place as the author's mother. What emerges is an account of the author from a mother's point of view, one Varble draws from Jane Clemens's notes, letters, and general recollections. This biography is more for a general audience than a scholarly one, with no documentation and only a brief bibliography.

249. Walker, Franklin. *Irreverent Pilgrims: Melville, Browne, and Mark Twain in the Holy Land.* Seattle: University of Washington Press, 1974.

In this study, Walker discusses Melville, Browne, and Twain and the different perspectives that these three select observers brought with them in their visits to the Holy Land. Of special note is Walker's comparison of Melville's attitudes and ideas with Twain's, which suggests that Twain had a deeper understanding of the religious significance of the Holy Land than he acknowledged in his *Innocents Abroad.*

250. Wilson, Rufus Rockwell, and Otilie Erickson Wilson. *New York in Literature.* Elmira, N.Y.: Primavera Press, 1947.

Although this book refers little to Mark Twain, on pages 336–50 the Wilsons do provide some background on Twain's courtship days with Olivia Langdon and his early association with Elisha Bliss. They also discuss the birth of Langdon, Clara, and Olivia Clemens, all born in Elmira, New York, and the many summers the Clemens family spent at Quarry Farm.

8

# Essay Collections

*The following collections focus on both the life and work of Mark Twain, some containing essential essays that have provided standard ways of viewing the author and others pointing toward a revision of critical standards. Collections based on particular works, such as the many on* Adventures of Huckleberry Finn, *have generally been left out. The emphasis here is on those collections that best enable an understanding of the author and his works.*

251. Anderson, Frederick, editor. *Mark Twain: The Critical Heritage.* London: Routledge and Kegan Paul; New York: Barnes and Noble, 1971.

This collection offers a selection of reviews and essays about Mark Twain and his works. Anderson's lengthy introduction sets the essays in proper context. All the essays were written while Twain was still alive or soon after his death. This collection provides a useful starting point for further investigation into Twain's life and the critical essays that form a basis for Twain scholarship. A couple of Twain's letters, one previously unpublished to Andrew Chatto, are included.

252. Bloom, Harold, editor. *Mark Twain: Modern Critical Views.* New York: Chelsea House Publishers, 1986.

The essays in this collection range from selections such as Bernard DeVoto's "Mark Twain and the Great Valley," taken from his 1946 *The Portable Mark Twain,* to Cleo McNelly Kearns's essay on "The Limits of Semiotics in *Huckleberry Finn*" (1986). Alfred Kazin's "Creatures of Circumstance: Mark Twain," adopted from his *An American Procession* (1984), is particularly suitable for those interested in Twain's life, showing as it does that he was intricately connected to his time and place, more driven by the circumstances of his context than in control of them. James M. Cox's "Life on the Mississippi," from his *The Mythologizing of Mark Twain,* links biography with myth, exposing the degree to which Twain wrote his own life story—which we continue to write, with the help of his works.

253. Budd, Louis J. *Critical Essays on Mark Twain, 1867–1910.* Boston: G. K. Hall and Company, 1983.

The first of two volumes, this book of essays is wide ranging and, as James Nagel points out in its opening pages, represents "the most comprehensive collection of criticism ever assembled" for its target years. What much of the early criticism reveals is that Mark Twain was himself as much a subject for examination as his works. Critics and reviewers found the author's life and career fascinating and regularly revised his image for the public. What developed were images of an author "contradictory enough to fit any biographical theory." In this collection, Twain's early critics, friends, and acquaintances expose the author as lecturer, editor, writer, funny man, family man, traveler, philosopher, political satirist, serious humorist, and emissary to the world. Budd's introduction provides a substantial discussion of the intricate interplay between biography and criticism.

254. Budd, Louis J. *Critical Essays on Mark Twain, 1910–1980.* Boston: G. K. Hall and Company, 1983.

This second volume in Budd's collection of essays on Mark Twain offers thirty essays written since the author's death. As with his introduction to the first volume in this collection, Budd again traces the reciprocal lines of influence between the portrait of Twain's life and career and the critical debates that developed around both. Some of the more illuminating essays that Budd presents along these lines are H. L. Mencken's "The Man Within," Fred Lewis Pattee's "On the Rating of Mark Twain," Robert Herrick's "Mark Twain and the American Tradition," John C. Gerber's "Mark Twain's Use of the Comic Pose," and Stanley Brodwin's "The Theology of Mark Twain: Banished Adam and the Bible."

255. Cardwell, Guy A., editor. *Discussions of Mark Twain.* Boston: D. C. Heath and Company, 1963.

This collection contains eighteen critical essays, all of which have been selected from books and periodicals. The essays range over a fifty-year period. Of note for biographical purposes are Stuart

P. Sherman's "Mark Twain, American," a short commemorative essay published in 1910, the year of Twain's death; Dixon Wecter's "The Idle Begins"; and Dwight MacDonald's "Mark Twain: An Unsentimental Journey." Sherman discusses Twain's religion, politics, and various occupations in his brief tribute and solidifies the author's image as an embodiment of American ideals; Wecter recalls Twain's younger days in Florida and Hannibal, Missouri; and MacDonald explores the "Mark Twain problem," the seeming split between the later and earlier Mark Twain.

256. Giddings, Robert, editor. *Mark Twain: A Sumptuous Variety.* London: Vision Press, 1985.

As its title suggests, this collection of essays contains a wide-ranging selection of essays. Those most substantially biographical in focus are Giddings's own essay, "Mark Twain and King Leopold of the Belgians"; William Kaufman's "The Comedic Stance: Sam Clemens, His Masquerade"; and Eric Mottram's "A Raft against Washington: Mark Twain's Criticism of America." Giddings discusses Twain's involvement with the international issues surrounding the exploration of the Congo; Kaufman writes about Mark Twain as a mask for Sam Clemens and his attacks on social and political abuses; and Mottram develops his portrait of Twain.

257. Hutchinson, Stuart, editor. *Mark Twain: Critical Assessments.* 4 vols. Banks near Robertsbridge, East Sussex: Helm Information, 1993.

The first volume of this four-volume collection is titled *The Biographical Responses,* and it contains selections from early biographical material, primarily from the work of Paine, Howells, and Clara Clemens. Volumes 2 through 4 offer an impressive range of critical responses to Twain and his work. Many of the essays, such as William Lyon Phelps's "Mark Twain," which was first published in the *North American Review* (1907), and Hamlin Hill's "Who Killed Mark Twain," first published in *American Literary Realism* (1974), offer diverse perspectives on Twain's life and his career.

258. Kesterson, David B. *Critics on Mark Twain: Readings in Literary Criticism.* Coral Gables, Fla.: University of Miami Press, 1973.

This book offers a "lively" selection of Twain criticism, a mix of favorable and unfavorable portraits extending from Twain's own time to this book's publication date, a century of critical study devoted to "a man and writer who above all remains an enigma in world literature." Kesterson divides the collection into four sections: "Critics on Mark Twain, 1882–1940," "Critics on Twain since 1940," "General Critical Evaluations," and "Critics on Specific Works." Particularly useful for Twain biography are those selections written by William Dean Howells, Joel Chandler Harris, and Joseph H. Twichell, all found in the first section. The pieces written by Robert Gay on "The Two Mark Twains" and by Edward Wagenknecht on "Some Classifications," found in the third section, are equally informative. All selections are excerpts from previously published articles and books.

259. Leary, Lewis. *Southern Excursions: Essays on Mark Twain and Others.* Baton Rouge: Louisiana State University Press, 1970.

The essays on Twain fill half this book, with the other half being devoted to the "others." Leary reviews Twain's life and provides a summary list of his own work and major critical statements about Twain. The essays most useful for a study of Twain's life are "Mark Twain and the Comic Spirit" and "The Bankruptcy of Mark Twain." The essays on Twain generally reveal the author as a psychologically wounded artist, a portrait that resembles the one Leary draws in *A Casebook on Mark Twain's Wound.*

260. Leary, Lewis, editor. *A Casebook on Mark Twain's Wound.* New York: Thomas Y. Crowell, 1962.

A collection of essays working from the assumption that Twain suffered, to one degree or another, from a fractured psyche. Van Wyck Brooks and Bernard DeVoto set the mood for this collection with contributors aligning themselves within, or somewhere between, Brooks's loosely Freudian claims about Twain's stunted creative potential and DeVoto's equally persuasive argument about Twain's genius as a frontier humorist.

261. Leonard, James S., Thomas S. Tenney, and Thadious M. Davis, editors. *Satire or Evasion: Black Perspectives on Huckleberry Finn.* Durham: Duke University Press, 1992.

Mark Twain's *Adventures of Huckleberry Finn* remains, as always, a controversial book. In the late twentieth century, the problems of Twain's depiction of Jim and of the author's racial understanding in general loom large. This set of essays directly faces this problem as the writers describe and examine Twain's racial attitudes and expressions as found in his most famous novel and as witnessed in his life. Black scholars contribute all the essays, which distinguishes this collection from other volumes devoted to *Huckleberry Finn* and provides for a spirited debate over Twain's often contradictory portraits of African Americans. In "Mark Twain and the Black Challenge," an essay written for this volume, Carmen Subryan fairly and clearly charts Twain's evolving attitudes toward African Americans, his southern background, inconsistent beliefs, and well-intentioned, though ambivalent, support of the plight of blacks in America. For further reading, an annotated and substantial list of relevant articles and books follows the essays.

262. Neider, Charles. *Mark Twain.* New York: Horizon Press, 1967.

The essays in this book originally appeared as introductions for editions of Mark Twain's works. Each essay singles out a particular area of Twain's life or pertinent biographical topic. In the essays, Neider discusses Twain's travels, his relations with the Russians, his attitudes toward censorship, as well his novels, essays, and autobiography.

263. Quirk, Tom, editor. *Coming to Grips with Huckleberry Finn: Essays on a Book, a Boy, and a Man.* Columbia: University of Missouri Press, 1993.

Many of the essays collected here were written and published before, but Quirk provides them in this volume as a focused effort to understand more of the mystery of Mark Twain through a continuing exploration of his most famous novel, *Adventures of Huckleberry Finn.* Quirk has arranged the essays loosely around the composition of Twain's book, which allows him to trace the history of its development within the complex life of its creator's imagination. Quirk's intent, then, is to supply readers with an unusually provocative entry point into the life of Twain's mind. His opening two chapters detail Twain's writing experiences with *Huckleberry Finn* and with the writing of his autobiography. In "Huckleberry Finn's Heirs," Quirk points to the facts and fiction surrounding the image of Mark Twain and to his continuing literary influence. One leaves this book with a better understanding of Twain's imaginative process and creative mind.

264. Robinson, Forrest G. *The Cambridge Companion to Mark Twain.* New York: Cambridge University Press, 1993.

This collection contains eleven essays, and its contributors represent some of the better-known critics in American literature and in Twain scholarship. Louis J. Budd, in "Mark Twain as an American Icon," discusses the prominent position of Twain's image, originally promoted by Twain himself, as it emerged throughout America to sell and support an ever-increasing number of products, projects, and programs. Shelley Fisher Fishkin offers a revised portrait of Twain and his relations with women in "Mark Twain and Women." And in "Mark Twain's Theology: The Gods of a Brevet Presbyterian," Stanley Brodwin evaluates Twain's religious sentiments in response to a series of beliefs and spiritual notions that emerged in the nineteenth century. Most of the essays reflect the 1990s critical preoccupation with developing both a cultural and personal narrative around an eminent figure.

265. Schmitter, Dean Morgan, editor. *Mark Twain: A Collection of Criticism.* New York: McGraw-Hill Book Company, 1974.

Schmitter divides this book of thirteen critical essays into two sections, the first containing essays that explore the different phases of Twain's life and thought, and the second, criticism of his major titles. Of note in the first section are Edward Wagenknecht's "The Matrix," which details Twain's literary career and cites the critics and professors who managed it; Howard Mumford Jones's "The Pessimism of Mark Twain," which situates Twain's thinking in the religious and philosophical ideas of his day; and John S. Tuckey's "Mark Twain's Later Dialogue: The Me and the Machine." Tuckey's essay is particularly important since it redraws the lines of study around Twain's later years by closely documenting his intellectual engagement with his final works, especially with the different versions of his *Mysterious Stranger* tales.

266. Scott, Arthur L., editor. *Mark Twain: Selected Criticism.* Dallas: Southern Methodist University Press, 1955.

According to its editor, this collection of thirty-four essays "presents the cream of Mark Twain criticism from its start in 1867 down to the present" (which is 1955 for this volume). A list of some of the book's contributors certainly supports such an assertion. Here readers will find essays by William Dean Howells, Archibald Henderson, Waldo Frank, Carl Van Doren, Constance Rourke, Granville Hicks, Edward Wagenknecht, Walter Blair, and Lionel Trilling. Van Wyck Brooks, Harvey Higgins, and Edward Reeder probe the dark corners of Twain's psyche and return with their slightly different portraits of a psychologically fractured artist, while Bernard DeVoto reintegrates the pieces left from such critical analysis by establishing the strength of Twain's frontier character. Whether examining Twain's secret or public self, his private or social being, the writers of these selected essays and reviews keep the focus on Twain and off of themselves, which makes this volume particularly useful for students and scholars just beginning their study of the author.

267. Sloane, David E. E. *Mark Twain's Humor.* New York: Garland Publishing, 1993.

This collection of essays focuses on Twain's literary reputation and growth as a comic artist. The essays are divided into three sections, covering Twain's early, middle, and late periods in relation to his development as a humorist. Many of the essays can be found in other collections, though some are new to this volume. Some that provide useful historical and biographical information are Will Clemens's "Mark Twain on the Lecture Platform," Edith Wyatt's "An Inspired Critic," Louis J. Budd's "A Curious Republican," and Michael Kiskis's "The Comic Voice in Mark Twain's Autobiography." Sloane offers a balanced collection of criticism and scholarship.

268. Smith, Henry Nash. *Mark Twain: A Collection of Critical Essays.* Englewood Cliffs, N.J.: Prentice-Hall, 1963.

In his introduction to this set of essays, Smith reviews the critical making of the man and writer that readers and the public have come to know as Mark Twain. He suggests that the primary problem for Twain critics lies in understanding the man himself and his relation to American culture. This remains true, to a large degree, decades after the publication of this collection. While Twain may not have been the representative American drawn by his earliest admirers, Smith points out that "the man and his career constitute an essential part" of an American past. The essays that fill the pages of this collection reveal that to be the case.

269. Sundquist, Eric J., editor. *Mark Twain: A Collection of Critical Essays.* Englewood Cliffs, N.J.: Prentice Hall, 1994.

In the introduction to this collection, Sundquist places Twain firmly within his cultural and historical moment. His effort points toward the general direction of each of the contributors as they, in turn, describe and explore the entangled strands of historical and literary influences that to some degree shaped Mark Twain and his work. For biographical purposes, the most useful may be Sundquist's own "Mark Twain and Homer Plessy," Richard Slotkin's "Mark Twain's Frontier: Hank Morgan's Last Stand," and Susan K. Gillman's "The Writer's Secret Life: Twain and the Art of Authorship."

270. Tuckey, John S. *Mark Twain's* The Mysterious Stranger *and the Critics.* Belmont, Calif.: Wadsworth Publishing Company, 1968.

Tuckey's collection of critical essays includes his own groundbreaking work on the circumstances surrounding Twain's last sustained piece of writing. In the selection taken from his *Mark Twain and Little Satan,* Tuckey sets the stage for a new appreciation of Twain's *Mysterious Stranger* manuscripts and a reassessment of the author's later years as a writer. This collection also includes the text of the 1916 version of *The Mysterious Stranger,* which soon after its publication would be exposed as a fragmented product of editorial mishandling.

# 9

# Papers, Projects, and Special Publications

*This chapter includes generally nonbook sources that have developed around Mark Twain or the groups and publications dedicated to a deeper appreciation of Twain and a further understanding of his work. A note must be given here about Twain's popularity on the Internet and World Wide Web resources: Numerous Web pages have been developed for the study and appreciation of Mark Twain, some offering the complete texts of his major works. Other websites offer historical and biographical information, while still others market Twain products. All deserve visiting, but only the most popular Internet site is included in this section. Entries are arranged alphabetically by source title.*

271. *American Literary Scholarship: An Annual.* Durham: Duke University Press.

This review of scholarship and criticism includes a special chapter each year for the work done on Mark Twain. Competent scholars, such as Alan Gribben, Tom Quirk, and Louis Budd, have written the chapters in different volumes. Although the coverage is selective, it nonetheless is balanced and wide ranging. The Twain chapters contain a special section on biographies, as well as sections on new editions and critical interpretations of Twain's works. A section on reference books is also included.

272. *The Fence Painter,* edited by Henry H. Sweets III.

Sponsored by the Mark Twain Home Foundation of Hannibal, Missouri, this is a bulletin of the Mark Twain Boyhood Home Associates. It focuses on events and activities at Mark Twain's Boyhood Home and museum in Hannibal, Missouri. All Twain enthusiasts will find it informative, however. Each issue usually includes an article on Twain or his family (often reprints from biographical or autobiographical material) that emphasizes facts and history rather than criticism and interpretation. Sweets, the museum's director, provides continuous updates on meetings, special events, and Twain exhibits. The publication is housed in the museum at 208 Hill Street, Hannibal, Missouri.

273. *Mark Twain Circular,* edited by James S. Leonard.

This periodical is published quarterly by the Mark Twain Circle of America. It maintains a selected list of the articles and reviews recently published on Mark Twain and provides brief annotations for the entries. The *Circular* also lists and describes the various meetings and conferences scheduled each year around the subject of Mark Twain, along with the requirements for attending and presenting papers at these events. The publication is housed in the English Department at The Citadel in Charleston, South Carolina.

274. *The Mark Twain Forum,* owned and managed by Kevin J. Bochynski.

Started by Taylor Roberts in 1992, this is an on-line Internet mailing list that provides a forum for a continuing conversation on the subject of Mark Twain. The *Forum* welcomes scholars and all who are interested in Mark Twain and encourages a continuing dialogue that nurtures a deeper understanding of Twain's work. Postings include queries, book reviews, calls for papers, and general announcements and discussions. Since hundreds of Twain scholars subscribe to this Internet group, the questions and concerns of *Forum* participants often lead to the discovery of useful facts and little-known sources of information. To subscribe, send the message "sub Twain-L" along with your full name to listserv@yorku.ca.

275. *The Mark Twain Journal,* edited by Thomas A. Tenney.

In 1936, this periodical began as *The Mark Twain Quarterly;* the title changed to *The Mark Twain Journal* in 1953. Throughout the years it has remained the primary publication for those devoted to the study of Mark Twain and his works. Issues include critical and historical essays and an update on Twain scholarship and related events. The *Journal* is housed in the English Department at The Citadel in South Carolina, but it should not be confused with the *Mark Twain Circular,* which shares its address only.

276. *The Mark Twain Papers,* Robert H. Hirst, general editor.

Hundreds of Mark Twain's papers were left in the care of the trustees of the author's estate. As Twain's official biographer, Albert Bigelow Paine was permitted access to all the documents, and he and Clara Clemens Samossoud, Twain's sole surviving daughter, kept close watch over their use until their deaths, restricting and inhibiting publication of the papers. These letters, notebooks, and autobiographical writings, then, as well as other bits and pieces of information, have to varying degrees been maintained or released by the trustees. The papers are currently housed at Berkeley and are being published as part of the Mark Twain Project in the *Mark Twain Papers* series by the University of California Press. Although some of the papers have been published in part, enough material remains to issue over twenty volumes of letters, a definitive autobiography, and at least two more volumes of Twain's notebook and journal entries.

277. The Mark Twain Project.

This is a project that has now taken on multiple tasks. Through its series of publications of the *Mark Twain Papers,* the project publishes scholarly editions of Twain's unpublished material—letters, notebooks, and literary pieces. The project also is responsible for the *Works of Mark Twain,* a series that will eventually include authoritative editions of all Twain's published works. The *Mark Twain Library,* the third addition to the Mark Twain Project's series of books, also provides a general readership with authoritative texts, but spares the reader much of the scholarly apparatus. Twenty-three volumes have been published by the Mark Twain Project; seventy volumes, in all, will be published. Aside from the publication of his notebooks, journals, and letters, the project has to date published the following major works in both scholarly and popular editions: *No. 44, The Mysterious Stranger; A Connecticut Yankee in King Arthur's Court; The Adventures of Tom Sawyer; Tom Sawyer Abroad; Tom Sawyer, Detective; The Prince and the Pauper; Adventures of Huckleberry Finn;* and *Roughing It.* Since 1980, the Mark Twain Project has been located in the Bancroft Library in Berkeley, California. Its series of books are published by the University of California Press.

278. *The Twainian,* edited by Richard Holmes.

This newsletter does not attempt to include the most recent waves of scholarship, but rather offers the often overlooked factual accounts or detailed information that continue to add to our knowledge of Mark Twain. What this newsletter loses in scope it gains in depth and focus. Each issue usually contains one or two articles that locate Twain within a historical context, plus a message from the editor. The newsletter is published by the Mark Twain Research Foundation and is mailed out from Culver-Stockton College in Canton, Missouri.

10

# Special Reference Sources

*The sources below provide in-depth information on Mark Twain and his works. They serve as special critical, biographical, and bibliographical guides.*

279. Gribben, Alan. *Mark Twain's Library: A Reconstruction.* 2 vols. Boston: G. K. Hall and Company, 1980.

Gribben has logged in his research miles for this book, having traveled back and forth across the United States in order to track down the more than seven hundred books that Twain once owned and that still exist. Working from these books; from Twain's letters, interviews, and notebook entries; and from a vast collection of primary and secondary sources, Gribben provides a collection of nearly five thousand titles, all of which represent Twain's range of reading. Catalog entries are arranged alphabetically by author's name when available, otherwise by title. Along with basic bibliographic information, Gribben describes Twain's markings and marginal comments and lists the current location of the book or other written material. Gribben's commentaries are especially useful. He often supplies a biographical context for Twain's reading habits, connects the reading material to the author's own works, or notes the possibility of literary influence. Also included is an annotated bibliography of previous studies done on Mark Twain's reading.

280. LeMaster, J. R., and James D. Wilson, editors. *The Mark Twain Encyclopedia.* New York: Garland Publishing, 1993.

This is an impressively complete reference book with over 740 entries relating to the life and works of Mark Twain. Each entry includes the name of its contributor, and many are written by respected scholars and critics. Given the wide sweep of this book's coverage, the entries are necessarily short, though some can be several pages in length when the topic requires detailed attention. A bibliography follows each entry, and the editors provide a substantially complete chronology and Clemens genealogy at the end of the encyclopedia. Little escapes notice in this book, which provides a guide to a vast amount of information about a wide range of topics concerning Mark Twain.

281. Long, E. Hudson. *Mark Twain Handbook.* New York: Hendricks House, 1957.

As part of the *Handbooks of American Literature* series, this volume provides easy access to some of the most significant studies of Mark Twain and his work. Long summarizes and evaluates selective articles and books, organizing his chapters around particular topics: "The Growth of Mark Twain Biography," "Backgrounds," "The Man of Letters," "Mind and Art," "Fundamental Ideas," and "Mark Twain's Place in Literature." His discussion within these topical frames usefully places Twain's work within its historical context, and Long suggests connections between Twain's life and its historical and literary background. Long's handbook, then, reads like a biography. It offers both biographical facts and an assessment of scholarship about the author's life and work. It also includes a chronological table of major events in Twain's life and publication dates of some of his most important works.

282. Long, E. Hudson, and J. R. LeMaster, editors. *The New Mark Twain Handbook.* New York: Garland Publishing, 1985.

Like the earlier *Mark Twain Handbook,* this book accounts for some of the most significant studies of Mark Twain. In the twenty-eight years separating the publication of these two handbooks, hundreds of books and articles were written about Twain and his work. If one is looking primarily for critical articles, then this volume adds little to its forerunner. Believing that most articles only expanded upon previous Twain scholarship, the editors chose to concentrate on book-length studies. The editors have also organized the handbook around the same topics, beginning with "The Growth of Mark Twain Scholarship" and ending with "Mark Twain's Place in American Literature." The chapters have been revised and to some degree rewritten around material from the earlier and newer edition.

283. Rasmussen, R. Kent. *Mark Twain A to Z: The Essential Reference to His Life and Writings*. New York: Oxford University Press, 1995.

No single reference book can cover the complex life and wide range of writings belonging to Mark Twain. Rasmussen acknowledges this in his introduction as he explains that his book focuses on "hard factual information" and not critical analysis and interpretation. While Rasmussen does rely on some secondary sources for his information, he finds many of his facts in Twain's own works. The book is arranged in alphabetical order by the names of real and fictional places and characters, by events and subjects related to Twain and his literary legacy, and by the titles of Twain's works. Entries for each title provide a brief discussion of the circumstances surrounding Twain's writing of a particular work and a detailed summary of the work itself. This book includes a detailed chronology that lists select facts about Twain's travels, residences, business ventures, and writing and publishing events, as well as a related literary and historical narrative.

284. Tenney, Thomas Asa. *Mark Twain: A Reference Guide.* Boston: G. K. Hall, 1977.

Organized by year beginning with 1858, Tenney provides an annotated guide to nearly all that has been written about Twain up until about a year before the publication of his own reference book. Each entry provides only a sentence or two but succinctly describes the book, review, or article at hand. Tenney also provides entries for essays and books that include letters, notebook entries, and other autobiographical material. Cross-references are given within entries for each critical work and point to related reviews and responses. Addenda include material overlooked and not contained in the guide proper.

285. Wilson, James D. *A Reader's Guide to the Short Stories of Mark Twain.* Boston: G. K. Hall, 1987.

This book serves as a critical introduction to Mark Twain's sixty-five short stories, providing more than just an analysis of each story. Along with details on each story's publication history, a critical appreciation, and a relevant bibliography, Wilson provides necessary historical and biographical information outlining the circumstances surrounding Twain's life at the time of a particular story's publication. The stories range across the years of Twain's career, from 1864 to 1904, and Wilson supplies an appendix that chronologically arranges the stories by publication date.

# Chronology

| | |
|---|---|
| 1835 | Samuel Langhorne Clemens born November 30, in Florida, Missouri, to John Marshall Clemens and Jane Lampton Clemens. |
| 1839 | Clemens family moves to Hannibal, Missouri. |
| 1840 | Begins his schooling. |
| 1847 | Works for the *Hannibal Gazette;* father dies of pneumonia on March 24. |
| 1848 | Works for Joseph Ament as an apprentice printer on the *Missouri Courier.* |
| 1849 | Finishes schooling. |
| 1850 | Works for his brother Orion's newspaper, the *Hannibal Western Union.* |
| 1851 | Publishes "A Gallant Fireman," his earliest known piece, in the *Hannibal Western Union.* |
| 1852 | Publishes "The Dandy Frightening the Squatter," his first publication in the East, in the Boston comic magazine *The Carpet-Bag.* |
| 1853–1856 | Is a wandering printer for several years; works at St. Louis, New York, Philadelphia, Keokuk (Iowa), and Cincinnati; publishes his "Thomas Jefferson Snodgrass" letters in the *Keokuk Daily Post.* |
| 1857 | Meets the steamboat pilot Horace Bixby, who agrees to accept him as his apprentice. |
| 1859 | Receives pilot's license on April 9. |

| | |
|---|---|
| 1861 | Concludes piloting career as Civil War interrupts the river trade; becomes a member of the St. Louis Masonic lodge; serves briefly as a Confederate volunteer near Marion County, Missouri; journeys westward with brother Orion to Carson City, Nevada. |
| 1862–3 | Works as reporter for the *Virginia City Territorial Enterprise;* adopts "Mark Twain" as a pseudonym for his "Carson City Letters"; meets Artemus Ward. |
| 1864 | Meets Bret Harte; writes for the *San Francisco Morning Call.* |
| 1865 | Pocket mines at Angel's Camp in California; publishes "Jim Smiley and His Jumping Frog" in the *New York Saturday Press* on November 18. |
| 1866 | Writes as a correspondent for the *Sacramento Daily Union* while in the Hawaiian Islands; begins his career as a paid lecturer on October 2, with a lecture on the "Sandwich Islands"; tours California and Nevada as a lecturer. |
| 1867 | Visits Europe and the Holy Land while writing travel letters for the *Alta California;* publishes *The Celebrated Jumping Frog of Calaveras County and Other Sketches;* meets Olivia Langdon in New York City. |
| 1868 | Lives in Washington, D.C.; works as secretary for Senator William Stewart of Nevada; lectures in California and Nevada. |
| 1869 | Meets William Dean Howells at the *Atlantic Monthly* offices in Boston; publishes *The Innocents Abroad.* |
| 1870 | Marries Olivia Langdon on February 2, in Elmira, New York; begins editorship at the *Buffalo Express;* son Langdon born on November 7. |

| | |
|---|---|
| 1871 | Moves to Nook Farm in Hartford, Connecticut; meets Thomas B. Aldrich; goes on an eastern lecture tour. |
| 1872 | Publishes *Roughing It;* daughter Olivia Susan ("Susy") is born on March 19; son Langdon dies on June 2; makes first visit to England. |
| 1873 | Writes and publishes *The Gilded Age* with Charles Dudley Warner; vacations with family in Europe; meets Robert Browning, Anthony Trollope, Lewis Carroll, and other British authors; secures a patent on his self-pasting scrapbook. |
| 1874 | Lectures in England; daughter Clara born on June 8; finishes and moves into Hartford house. |
| 1875 | Publishes "Old Times on the Mississippi" as seven installments in the *Atlantic Monthly.* |
| 1876 | Publishes *The Adventures of Tom Sawyer;* publishes "Facts Concerning a Recent Carnival of Crime in Connecticut" in the *Atlantic Monthly.* |
| 1877 | Travels to Bermuda with Joseph Twichell; gives generally ill-received Whittier Birthday Speech in Boston. |
| 1878–1879 | Lives and travels with family in Europe; lectures at Heidelberg University. |
| 1880 | Makes initial investment in Paige compositor (typesetting machine); daughter Jean born on July 26; publishes *A Tramp Abroad.* |
| 1881 | Meets G. W. Cable; publishes *The Prince and the Pauper.* |
| 1882 | Visits Hannibal while traveling on the Mississippi. |
| 1883 | Publishes *Life on the Mississippi;* invents a history game. |

| | |
|---|---|
| 1884 | Travels and lectures with G. W. Cable; visits Ulysses S. Grant in New York; establishes the publishing firm of Charles L. Webster and Company; takes bicycle riding lessons; becomes a member of the London-based Society for Psychical Research; publishes London edition of *Adventures of Huckleberry Finn.* |
| 1885–1886 | Publishes *Adventures of Huckleberry Finn* and the first volume of Grant's *Memoirs;* visits Hannibal; speaks before a Senate committee on copyright laws. |
| 1888 | Meets Robert Louis Stevenson in New York City; receives an honorary master of arts degree from Yale University. |
| 1889 | Meets Rudyard Kipling in Elmira; publishes *A Connecticut Yankee in King Arthur's Court.* |
| 1890 | Meets Edward Bellamy at Hartford; mother Jane Lampton Clemens dies on October 27; mother-in-law dies on November 28; buys all rights to the Paige compositor. |
| 1891 | Leaves Hartford and takes family to Europe for a nearly ten-year stay; frequents European health spas; begins marketing "Mark Twain's Memory Builder"; publishes personal observations on psychic phenomena in "Mental Telegraphy." |
| 1892 | Meets William James while vacationing in Florence, Italy; publishes *The American Claimant.* |
| 1894 | Appoints H. H. Rogers as his financial manager. Declares bankruptcy; publishes *The Tragedy of Pudd'nhead Wilson.* |
| 1895 | Begins a world lecture tour, which would take him as far away as Australia and New Zealand. |
| 1896 | Suffers death of daughter Susy on August 18; publishes *Personal Recollections of Joan of Arc.* |

| | |
|---|---|
| 1897 | Publishes *Following the Equator;* begins work on versions of *The Mysterious Stranger.* |
| 1898 | Pays off his creditors; vacations in Vienna; comes into contact with Sigmund Freud. |
| 1899 | Summers in Sanna, Sweden; meets Booker T. Washington; publishes "The Man That Corrupted Hadleyburg." |
| 1900 | Meets W. E. H. Lecky; returns to the United States; lives in New York City; introduces Winston Churchill to a New York City audience; speaks out against imperialism. |
| 1901 | Receives honorary degree of doctor of literature from Yale University; publishes "To the Person Sitting in Darkness" in the February issue of the *North American Review;* meets Albert Bigelow Paine. |
| 1902 | Pays his last visit to Hannibal; receives an honorary doctorate degree from the University of Missouri; invests in Plasmon, a powdered-milk health product; works on what many consider his final version of his mysterious stranger tale, *No. 44, The Mysterious Stranger.* |
| 1903 | Sells Hartford house; takes family to Italy for wife's health. |
| 1904 | Olivia Langdon Clemens dies in Italy on June 5; moves back to New York City. |
| 1906 | Publishes privately *What Is Man?;* visits Washington, D.C., and speaks before congressional committees on copyright laws; meets H. G. Wells; begins donning white suits for public display. |
| 1907 | Vacations in Bermuda with his close friend Joseph Twichell and personal secretary Isabel Lyon; publishes *Christian Science;* receives an honorary doctor of laws degree from Oxford. |

1908 Makes two separate visits to Bermuda, one with H. H. Rogers; begins a group for young girls to be known as the "Aquarium"; moves into his "Stormfield" home at Redding, Connecticut; forms the Mark Twain Company to control and protect his literary property.

1909 Publishes *Extract from Captain Stormfield's Visit to Heaven;* visits Bermuda with Albert Bigelow Paine; daughter Jean dies at Stormfield on Christmas Eve.

1910 Makes last trip to Bermuda for health reasons and returns on April 12; dies of heart failure at his Stormfield home on April 21; laid to rest in the family plot in Elmira, New York.

# Select Listing of Mark Twain's Books

1867 *The Celebrated Jumping Frog of Calaveras County and Other Sketches*

1869 *The Innocents Abroad, or The New Pilgrim's Progress: Being Some Account of the Steamship* Quaker City*'s Pleasure Excursion to Europe and the Holy Land.*

1871 *Mark Twain's (Burlesque) Autobiography and First Romance*

1872 *Roughing It*

1874 *The Gilded Age: A Tale of To-day*

1875 *Sketches New and Old*

1876 *The Adventures of Tom Sawyer*

1877 *A True Story and the Recent Carnival of Crime*

1880 *A Tramp Abroad*

1881 *The Prince and the Pauper*

1882 *The Stolen White Elephant, Etc.*

1883 *Life on the Mississippi*

1885 *Adventures of Huckleberry Finn*

1889 *A Connecticut Yankee in King Arthur's Court*

1892 *The American Claimant*

1893 *The 1,000,000 Bank-Note and Other New Stories*

| | |
|---|---|
| 1894 | *Pudd'nhead Wilson and Those Extraordinary Twins* |
| 1896 | *Personal Recollections of Joan of Arc* |
| 1897 | *Following the Equator* |
| 1898 | *More Tramps Abroad* |
| 1899 | *Literary Essays* |
| 1900 | *The Man that Corrupted Hadleyburg and Other Stories and Essays* |
| 1904 | *Extracts from Adam's Diary* |
| 1906 | *Eve's Diary* |
| | *What Is Man?* |
| 1907 | *Christian Science* |
| 1909 | *Extracts from Captain Stormfield's Visit to Heaven* |

---

*Posthumous Publications*

| | |
|---|---|
| 1916 | *The Mysterious Stranger, A Romance* |
| 1962 | *Letters from the Earth* |
| 1967 | *Mark Twain's Which Was the Dream? and Other Symbolic Writings of the Later Years* |
| 1969 | *Mark Twain's* Mysterious Stranger *Manuscripts* |
| 1972 | *Mark Twain's Fables of Man* |
| 1973 | *What Is Man? and Other Philosophical Writings* |

# Index to Authors, Editors, and Compilers

*Names are indexed to relevant entry numbers.*

# Index to Titles

*Titles are indexed by entry numbers.*

# Index to Subjects

*Subjects are indexed by entry numbers.*

# About the Author

Jason Gary Horn is an assistant professor of English and chair of the Division of Humanities at Gordon College in Barnesville, Georgia. He has published several articles on Mark Twain and other American literary figures and is the author of *Mark Twain and William James: Crafting a Free Self,* which explores Twain's religious psychology and philosophical temperament.